Korean
Homestyle
COOKING

89 Classic Recipes
From Barbecue and Bibimbap to Kimchi and Japchae

Hatsue Shigenobu

T0160687

TUTTLE Publishing
Tokyo | Rutland, Vermont | Singapore

CONTENTS

First, let's learn the basics in Chapter 1!

Then we can make delicious Korean meals. ♪

Recipes anyone can make!

Delicious Korean Meals You Can Cook at Home!

Korean cuisine pairs well with white rice, and it's a great way to eat lots of vegetables with meat and seafood—it not only tastes good, it's also good for you! It's a pleasure to be able to create these dishes at home, instead of just enjoying them in restaurants. Perhaps you feel hesitant to make them yourself, thinking that you need special ingredients or kitchen utensils. What if you could make Korean recipes with ingredients found in a regular supermarket and the pots and pans you already own? Most of the recipes in this book are that simple. Once you get used to making those dishes, you can look for less familiar ingredients in specialty shops.

Now, let's get started!

Nutritious! Energizing!
Add Korean homestyle dishes to your repertoire!

Main
Galbi Short-rib Patties
page 58

Main dishes and sides with plenty of meat, fish and vegetables; soups that are gentle on the body . . . Korean cooking naturally helps you feel energized. It's surprisingly easy to create the authentic home-cooked flavors with everyday ingredients. Master the skills you need with this book, adopt these recipes into your regular meal rotation, and get a boost from this unique cuisine!

Galbi Patties Combo

Side

Tomato
Kimchi
page 86

Bean Sprout
Soup
page 111

Soup

Well-balanced Korean meals

Authentic Korean cuisine includes not only a main dish, but also soup, white rice, and multiple side dishes like kimchi lined up on the table. Korean cooks emphasize this balance.

Side

Korean Potato Salad page 92

Sweet & Salty Sardines with Green Bell Pepper page 89

Side

Delicious Korean Meal #2
Combines sweet and salty flavors, staples of Korean cooking!

Bulgogi Combo

Main

Bulgogi Soy-
marinated Beef
with Spring Onions
page 26

Soup

Wakame
Seaweed
Soup
page 109

Enjoy cooking Korean at home!

Korean cooking often involves eating various ingredients and sauces together. With one finishing touch before eating, your recipes can closely replicate the flavors of authentic Korean cuisine.

In the well-known dish Bibimbap, the *bibim* means "mixed" and the *bap* means "rice." This is just one of many Korean foods that you mix up well just before eating. By thoroughly combining everything in the dish, the flavors of the ingredients and sauce mingle and become one, making it taste even better.

Mix

This is an example of Bibimbap that has been thoroughly mixed. The ingredients and seasonings have been evenly blended together.

Mix these foods

- **Bibimbap Rice Bowls Topped with Vegetables and Meat**—page 24
- **Muchim Grilled Beef Salad**—page 94
- **Chilled Buckwheat Noodles with Toppings**—page 126

In Korea, there is a style of eating called *ssam,* meaning "wrapped," where meat and other fillings are wrapped in vegetables. Typically, ingredients like kimchi and sauces are wrapped together in some kind of leafy vegetable like lettuce, perilla leaves, cabbage leaves, or another type of leafy vegetable. Wraps can also be enjoyed with stir-fries and can help you polish off your leftovers. They combine a variety of flavors and are fun to enjoy with friends and easy to pop into your mouth . . . it's a healthy style of eating with many benefits!

Wrap

Wrap these foods

- **Samgyeopsal Grilled Pork Belly**—page 36
- **Galbi Short-rib Patties**—page 58
- **Simmered Pork Belly**—page 60

You can wrap pieces of Galbi Patties in red-leaf lettuce to make it easy to eat. You can also use Japanese shiso leaves instead of Korean perilla leaves because they have a very similar flavor.

Why should we eat Korean food more often?

Korean food is not just delicious. I've listed three other reasons to add some Korean dishes to your everyday meals.

3 Reasons Korean Dishes are Perfect for Home Cooking

1 *They are healthy and full of vegetables!*

Korean cooking may have a reputation for leaning heavily on meat, but it actually uses a lot of vegetables. Whether you're serving Namul or Kimchi as an appetizer or creating vegetable wraps for your meat dishes, Korean cooking has lots of vegetables prepared in many different ways. By learning to make Korean homestyle recipes, you can learn new ways to make vegetables taste delicious—making it easier to incorporate more of them in your diet.

Three-color Namul Salad—page 48

For example

Japchae Glass Noodles with Fresh Vegetables—page 30

It's wonderful to be able to enjoy so many vegetables!

Stir-fried Vegetables and Squid with Bonito Flakes—page 74

2 Spices, condiments and fermented foods promote health!

The foundation of Korean culinary culture is "five tastes, five colors." The five tastes are spicy, sweet, sour, salty and bitter, and the five colors are green, red, yellow, white and black. To arrange these five tastes and five colors on the table in a balanced way, condiments called *yangnyeom* are indispensable. Korean food combines spices like fiery chili peppers and a variety of fermented condiments like kimchi and bean paste that contain probiotics and promote digestive health. This style of cooking puts into practice the ancient idea that herbal medicines and foods share the same origin.

Bulgogi Soy-marinated Beef with Spring Onions —page 26

For example

Hearty Kimchi Jjigae Stew—page 104

Kimchi and veggies will boost your stamina!

3 Add flavor quickly with sauces!

Korean cooking uses sauces made from a mixture of seasonings, condiments and so on. If you prepare the basic sauces ahead of time, you can whip up delicious meals quickly and easily. By mixing several kinds of sauces, you'll create a depth of flavor the way a skilled chef does. In this book, I introduce sauces that can be prepared in advance and stored for convenient use in a variety of recipes (see page 18).

Great for saving time!

Buchimgae Seafood Pancakes—page 32

For example

Fresh Tuna with Spicy Gochujang Dressing—page 78

In this book, I have compiled as many recipes that use familiar ingredients as possible. These are easy for beginners to make at home using a few simple seasonings. Try them for yourself!

The Korean Pantry: Key Spices and Ingredients

Here, I introduce the frequently used ingredients that are representative of Korean cooking. I also share tips for using each one.

Chili Peppers

Chili peppers are frequently used to give Korean food some heat. We use fresh peppers or ones that have been dried and crushed. Crushed peppers are used for different purposes, depending on how finely they are ground.

(Fresh Chili Peppers)
Korean chili peppers are rather mild

Korean chili peppers are mild compared to Thai chilis, which can be substituted, but you may want to reduce the quantity. Korean peppers have about the same heat as large jalapeños. Cut them up to use them in cooking or as a garnish. Korean chili peppers are either green or red; the green ones are slightly hotter.

(Korean Red Chili Pepper (*gochugaru*))
Bring some heat to your cooking!

Red chili peppers that have been dried and ground more coarsely than in red pepper powder. This is used in making Kimchi and in stir-fries. If you cannot get Gochugaru, use Ground Pepper Powder instead.

(Red Chili Pepper Threads)
Add some vibrant color to your dish

These are red chili peppers that have been dried and cut into slender threads. They are not very spicy, but they have a beautiful color, so they are frequently used as a garnish.

(Ground Pepper Powder)
Gently spice up your soups and stews

This powder is made of chili peppers that have been dried and finely ground. The powder is relatively mild compared to Gochugaru, so this red pepper powder is often used to season soups and stews. It is similar to ground red pepper normally found in supermarkets, but has a richer, smoky flavor.

Gochujang Red Chili Bean Paste

The unique spicy-sweet taste and red color of Korean chili peppers make this an iconic condiment. Whether you mix it straight into your Bibimbap or use it to flavor a stir-fry, there are countless ways to enjoy this red chili bean paste.

An essential part of Korean cooking, *gochujang* is a type of fermented soybean paste with sugar and red pepper powder added. It is made with soybeans and glutinous rice, then fermented. *Gochujang* isn't just spicy; it's also rich and sweet, so it often plays a role in flavoring hot-pots and side dishes with dressings.

Kimchi

Kimchi is a spicy pickled and fermented vegetable dish that is widely used as a cooking ingredient and a seasoning as well as being eaten as a side dish on its own. Well-aged fermented kimchi is slightly more sour and used in many Korean foods to create a savory flavor.

Preserving Kimchi

Changes in temperature affect the fermentation and taste

Because the temperature in the refrigerator tends to be warmer near the door, fermentation will happen faster in that area and the taste will change. If you prefer a fresh flavor, divide the kimchi so that you have some to use in the short term and put the rest in the back of the refrigerator. As the acidity increases in well-aged, fermented kimchi, the savoriness will increase as well.

Kimchi is a central dish in Korean cuisine. It's made by salting napa cabbage and daikon radish, and then allowing them to ferment naturally with seasonings like red pepper powder, garlic and fish sauce or fermented shrimp. You can use kimchi in stews and stir-fries, and also enjoy it as a condiment or side dish.

Leafy Salad Vegetables

Leafy vegetables are often used as wraps for meat and other fillings. If you can't get certain vegetables in your area, you can use local greens as a substitute.

Japanese green shiso leaves have a similar flavor to Korean perilla, and make an excellent substitute!

Korean Perilla Leaves
Large, thick leaves

Korean perilla is a plant belonging to the mint family. The sturdy leaves characteristic of this species bring a uniquely appetizing flavor to a meal. In addition to being used as a wrap, the leaves can also be pickled in soy sauce.

Lettuce Leaves
A common wrap for grilled meats

Koreans love to roll up cooked pieces of meat in lettuce leaves. In Korea, they use *sangchu* lettuce but you can substitute red-leaf or green-leaf lettuces instead.

Where can I buy Korean ingredients?

Kimchi and Gochujang are popular enough in the United States that it's possible to find them in larger grocery stores, but some other ingredients may be more difficult to obtain. If a city near you has an Asian food market, most commonly used Korean ingredients should be available there, and there are import and specialty food shops that might be helpful as well. If there are no such shops in your area, try ordering the ingredients online.

A Quick Guide to Korean Ingredients and Utensils

The following ingredients appear in the recipes in this book.

Sesame oil

Very fragrant with a full-bodied taste

Sesame oil that is made in Korea has a stronger smell and richer taste than sesame oil made in Japan, China or elsewhere.

Dried sardine stock powder

This is your ally when you don't have much time

Dried sardine stock is often used in Korean soups, along with beef stock. You can make it at home (see page 19), but store-bought stock is a convenient alternative when you're short on time. You can also use dashi stock powder as a substitute although the taste is different. Vegetable stock powder can also be substituted.

Beef stock powder

Get that classic taste without all the work

Beef stock powder extracts the savory flavor of beef, and is popular in Korea. It can be salty, so check the taste and adjust the other seasonings accordingly. You can also use canned or packaged beef stock.

Naemyeong (cold buckwheat noodles)

Chewy with a firm texture

Koreans use these noodles in cold dishes. They are made by adding thickener to buckwheat flour. The smooth, chewy, elastic texture is a unique characteristic of this noodle. You can use Japanese soba or Chinese somen wheat noodles as a substitute, or fine angel hair pasta.

Korean glass noodles

These springy noodles won't fall apart when you cook them

On the left are mung bean glass noodles, and on the right are Korean glass noodles. You can see the difference in thickness and color.

Korean glass noodles are made from sweet potato starch, which makes them thick, highly elastic and chewy. They are used in stir-fried dishes like Japchae and in hot pots. You can use mung bean glass noodles as a substitute.

Salted fermented shrimp

A very salty and savory seasoning

This seasoning is made by curing tiny shrimp in salt and aging them. The strong salty and savory taste is essential for making kimchi and flavoring stir-fries and soups. Similar fermented baby shrimp are used in Thai, Vietnamese and Malaysian cooking and any of those can be used as a substitute. Or, you can add fermented fish sauce to tiny fresh or cooked shrimp.

Pine nuts

A highly nutritious garnish

Pine nuts are often used as a topping for Korean dishes. Eighty percent of the fats are unsaturated fatty acids, which are said to be healthy. Pine nuts are also high in dietary fiber, and are known to have health and beauty benefits. They are used in Italian cooking and are widely available.

Gim seasoned laver

The combination of the seaweed, sesame and salt taste is delicious

These sheets of laver seaweed are fragrantly seasoned with sesame oil and salt. Oils other than sesame oil, such as perilla oil and olive oil, are also used. Gim has a variety of uses, as it can be eaten as it is or used as a wrap or in salads.

Korean rice cakes

These rice flour cakes come in a variety of shapes and sizes

The long, thin *tteok-bokki* rice cakes (above right) are coated in sweet and spicy sauce. *Tteok* (above left) is the thinly sliced round rice cakes used in soup. They are made with a mixture of glutinous and non-glutinous rice flours and they are very firm so they don't fall apart in soups. You can use seitan as a substitute.

Makgeolli rice wine

A mildly sweet and tangy wine

This wine is made from glutinous rice, regular rice, wheat flour and other ingredients. It is mildly sweet and has a refreshing astringency. You can substitute sake, rice wine or cooking sherry.

Wood-ear mushrooms

Deliciously crunchy

These mushrooms have a crunchy texture, and are black or brown in color. They are rich in iron and vitamins. Dried mushrooms should be rehydrated in water before being used. You can use shiitake mushrooms as a substitute.

Wolf berries (Goji)

Tiny red berries that look great and are very healthy

These red berries are often used as a garnish or topping. Goji berries are known as a traditional medicinal ingredient, and contain many vitamins and minerals. You can use dried cranberries as a substitute.

Great for an aromatic, fried finish: stone bowls and *jeongol* pots

Chopsticks and spoons come as a set in most kitchens: *jeotgarak* and *sutgarak*

Korean utensils and cooking equipment

Having these in your kitchen will make it feel like a real Korean kitchen

The stone pot used for Bibimbap (pictured on the left), made from natural stone, holds heat exceptionally well. *Jeongol* (pictured on the right) is a relatively shallow frying pan used for Korean hot-pot dishes. Because it is wide, it can hold a lot of ingredients, making it convenient to serve food at the table for a group of people. Other shallow pots, like a Japanese *sukiyaki* pot or a casserole pot, can be used as a substitute for the *jeongol*.

In Korea, chopsticks (called *jeotgarak*) and a long spoon (called *sutgarak*) come as a set. Picking up rice or soup bowls with your hand is considered bad manners in Korea, so the chopsticks and spoons are longer in Korea than they are in Japan or China, because your bowl should remain on the table at all times and you need to reach the serving dishes at the center of the table with these.

If you always have some sauce on hand that you've mixed up from seasonings and spices, you can make a delicious Korean dish in a snap! All of the ingredients are listed in convenient amounts. You just have to blend them together.

Simple and Convenient Homemade Sauces and Stocks

Sauces and stocks are often used in Korean cooking. They're easy to make—just combine all ingredients and mix to blend. They're also easy to use and store in the fridge.

Spicy Dipping Sauce

Keep in refrigerator
Use within 1 month

This chili pepper sauce is hot but very tasty!

3 tablespoons finely chopped fresh chili peppers (red and green)
⅓ cup (80 ml) soy sauce
2 tablespoons sugar
2 tablespoons sesame oil

How to use it:
- As a dipping sauce for dishes like Buchimgae (page 32) and assorted Jeon (page 72)
- As a dipping sauce for steamed fish or hot-pot morsels

Super Tasty Sauce

Elevate your sauce by adding more seasonings and spices!

½ teaspoon minced garlic
1 tablespoon toasted white sesame seeds
2-in (5-cm) length green onion (scallion), white part only, finely chopped
1 teaspoon each finely chopped fresh red and green chili peppers
1 teaspoon Korean ground pepper powder
½ cup (125 ml) soy sauce
1 tablespoon rice vinegar
1 tablespoon sesame oil
2 teaspoons sugar

Keep in refrigerator
Use within 1 month

How to use it:
- As a sauce for the same dishes as Spicy Dipping Sauce, and on dishes like Mixed Rice with Ground Beef and Bean Sprouts (page 124)

Spicy Bean Paste Sauce

Keep in refrigerator
Use within 2 months

Refreshingly sweet and spicy sauce with a touch of acidity

6 tablespoons *gochujang* red chili bean paste
3 tablespoons soy sauce
2 tablespoons sesame oil
2 tablespoons sugar
2 tablespoons rice vinegar

How to use it:
- On Fresh Tuna with Spicy Gochujang Dressing (page 78), Spicy Gochujang Caprese Salad (page 93), sashimi, seasoned vegetables, salads, stir-fries, etc.

Korean-style Fish Stock

A variety of stocks—beef, chicken and sardine, among others—are used in Korea. Dried sardine stock is especially easy: it only involves soaking the sardines in water and simmering to extract the flavor! You can easily make a hearty, flavorful stock right at home. (Sardine stock powder and dashi stock powder are also available and are convenient substitutes.)

Ingredients and directions

1 Prep and Soak
Remove the heads from ½ cup (30 g) small dried sardines. Place them in a saucepan with 4 cups (1 liter) water, and let stand for 30 minutes.

2 Boil
Bring the broth to a boil over medium heat, skimming the foam off the top. Lower the heat and let simmer for 2 to 3 minutes.

3 Strain
Remove from heat and allow to cool briefly, then strain through a fine mesh sieve lined with paper towel, cheesecloth or similar material. That's it!

4 Store
Sardine stock will last 2 days in the refrigerator, or up to a month in the freezer if well sealed.

How to use it:
- In dishes like Sundubu-Jjigae (page 28) and Wakame Seaweed Soup (page 109), or as a base in hot pots and soups.

How to use this book to make cooking at home a snap!

Stir-fried Dak-galbi Chicken with Cheese

Cover your Dak-galbi in melted cheese! This style is very popular in Korea now, and you can easily make it at home!

[Serves 4]
1 recipe Dak-galbi (see pages 40–41), divided
½ to ¾ cup (60 to 75 g) grated pizza cheese (mozzarella or provolone)

┤ Easy & Delicious Tip ├
Use a tabletop burner to keep the cheese warm
Once you shut off the heat, the melted cheese will soon begin to harden and the dish will become less appetizing. I recommend keeping the pan warm over a portable burner on the table and serve the melty Dak-galbi right out of the pan like a fondue!

Cooking tips at a glance

The "Easy & Delicious Tips" (in Chapter 1) and the "Tips" columns (in Chapters 2–6) will offer tips and tricks that aren't in the recipe steps. These will help you make the dishes taste even better.

Classic Korean Dish 9

Frying Pan — Total time 35 min
* Not including marinating time

Required cookware is listed separately for quick reference

You can instantly tell from the icon whether you'll be using a pot, frying pan, microwave, small grill, etc.

When it's this easy, anyone can cook it!

Estimated cooking times

Knowing the required cooking time is important to many people, so this information is listed for every recipe.

As I introduce classic Korean dishes in Chapter 1, I'll clearly explain each step in the process and include pictures. I'll be with you every step of the way, so just relax and get cooking!

How to read the recipes

° Each recipe will specify the number of servings made with the given amount of ingredients.

° The steps to prepare vegetables will be listed assuming the vegetables have already been washed. There are cases where steps like peeling, cutting off the roots, and removing the core will be omitted.

° You can use stock powder where recipes call for soup stock, but the salt content is usually higher in store-bought powders, so check the taste of your stock and adjust the other seasonings accordingly. See "Korean-style Fish Stock" recipe on page 19 to make your own.

° If the recipe doesn't call for fresh chili peppers, you can use a dried chili pepper product.

° If the recipe doesn't specify, "soy sauce" refers to the normal soy sauce; "flour" refers to cake flour; and "sugar" means superfine sugar.

° The "total time" listed is an estimate of how long the recipe will take to prepare. The time needed to rehydrate, cool, or pickle the ingredients may not be included.

Cookware and measurements

° 1 teaspoon = 5 ml; 1 tablespoon = 15 ml.

° If a recipe calls for a frying pan, use a non-stick one (or one that is well seasoned).

° Microwave heating times are based on a 600-watt appliance. For a 500-watt microwave, multiply the time by 1.2. Toaster oven heating times are based on a 1000-watt model. Different models vary, so check your food as it heats and make adjustments as needed.

43

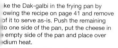

step 1 Make the Dak-galbi

...ke the Dak-galbi in the frying pan by ...owing the recipe on page 41 and remove ...f it to serve as-is. Push the remaining ...o one side of the pan, put the cheese in ... empty side of the pan and place over ...dium heat.

【 ◗◗◗ Medium heat 】

You can enjoy two different tastes by eating a third of the Dak-galbi recipe (pages 40–41) as-is, and by adding cheese to the rest.

step 2 Add the finishing touch

When the cheese is melted, lower the heat and mix everything together to serve.

【 ◗◗◗ Low heat 】

The last stop for leftover Dak-galbi is to turn it into Dak-galbi fried rice!

Waste not! Instead of throwing away your leftover Dak-galbi, make it into fried rice like they do in Korea.

Ingredients and directions

For about ¼ of a recipe of Dak-galbi: Cut the leftover chicken into small bite-size pieces with kitchen scissors; tear up a sheet of *nori* seaweed. Heat 2 teaspoons of sesame oil in a frying pan. Add 2 cups (400 g) of cooked white rice, the chicken and the *nori*. Stir-fry together over medium heat for 3 minutes. Level the surface of the rice and leave over low heat for 1 to 2 minutes. The rice is especially tasty when it gets a little crispy on the bottom.

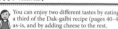

Helpful tips are provided in boxes

These boxes contain an explanation for points that are easy to overlook in the directions. They will provide extra detail about parts that might trip you up.

Supplementary columns introduce related recipes or information about the ingredients

The "More to enjoy! A touch of creativity" column introduces ways to experiment with a recipe, and the "Ingredient Note" column explains ingredients and seasonings that might be new to you. Reading these columns helps you enjoy your cooking experience even more.

Let's start with
the most popular
Korean dishes!

Effortlessly create these flavors at home!

Classic Korean Dishes

It's such a shame that many people are under the impression that Korean food can only be enjoyed in a restaurant! Well-known dishes like Bibimbap, Buchimgae and Bulgogi are all examples of Korean home cooking. I've composed 14 recipes so you can easily create these authentic flavors at home. Try to incorporate them into your everyday diet!

Saucepan   Frying Pan   Total time 20 min

Bibimbap Rice Bowls Topped with Vegetables and Meat

Add colorful seasoned vegetables, or *namul*, on top for a highly nutritious meal!
In Korean cooking, this is a classic among classics.

[Serves 4]

1 medium carrot
1 small zucchini
3 cups (300 g) bean sprouts
⅓ cup (75 g) cooked Asian royal
    fern (see page 45) or spinach
3 tablespoons sesame oil, divided
Ⓐ 2 teaspoons salt
   ⅛ teaspoon sugar

1 lb (450 g) ground beef or ground pork
Ⓑ 2 teaspoons soy sauce
   2 teaspoons sugar
   ½ teaspoon minced garlic
4 cups (800 g) warm white rice
4 egg yolks or sunny-side-up eggs
2 tablespoons pine nuts
2–3 tablespoons *gochujang* red chili
    bean paste

⌐ Easy & Delicious Tip ⌐
**Mix well to enhance
the flavor!**

In Korean, *bibim* means
"to mix" and *bap* means
"rice." Combine everything
well to achieve the height
of flavor.

If you can't find Asian royal
fern, use blanched mild
greens instead.

step 1 Cut the vegetables

Cut the carrot into matchsticks with a mandoline, or large box grater, or knife. Use a knife to cut the zucchini into slivers as shown.

【 ◆◆◆ Medium heat 】

step 2 Cook the vegetables

Remove the roots from the bean sprouts and cut the fern into 2-in (5-cm) pieces. (If using spinach, remove the stems.) Blanch the bean sprouts for 2–3 minutes in boiling water in the saucepan until tender. Briefly blanch the fern or spinach. Drain well and allow to cool, then squeeze out the remaining water.

Heat 1 tablespoon of the sesame oil in a frying pan over medium heat. Add the carrot and stir-fry for 1 or 2 minutes until soft, then transfer to a bowl. Heat another 1 tablespoon of the sesame oil and stir-fry the zucchini until soft, placing in a separate bowl.

【 ◆◆◆ Medium heat 】

You can use the same seasoning for different vegetables!

step 3 Add seasoning

Mix the salt and sugar from **Ⓐ** and divide into four parts. Stir one portion into each vegetable.

【 ◆◆◆ Medium heat 】

step 4 Stir-fry the meat

Heat the remaining 1 tablespoon sesame oil in a frying pan over medium heat. Add the ground meat and cook for 2 to 3 minutes. When the meat separates, mix in the soy sauce, sugar and garlic from **Ⓑ**.

Arrange the ingredients by color to create a balanced and beautiful dish.

step 5 Arrange for serving

Divide the rice equally among four large, shallow bowls. Divide the vegetables and meat into quarters and arrange separately over the rice. Top each serving with an egg yolk. Scatter pine nuts over each bowl and garnish with *gochujang*, then serve. Have guests mix all the ingredients together thoroughly before eating.

Frying
Pan

Total time
15 min

Bulgogi Soy-marinated Beef with Spring Onions

Big portions loaded with meat and vegetables! Sweet and spicy Korean BBQ.

[Serves 4]

4 green onions (scallions)
Small bunch chives
7 oz (200 g) *enoki* mushrooms or
   button mushrooms
1 fresh chili pepper
1½ lbs (675 g) beef, thinly sliced

Ⓐ ½ apple or pear, peeled and
   finely grated
4 tablespoons soy sauce
2 tablespoons honey
2 tablespoons sesame oil
2 teaspoons minced garlic
2 teaspoons peeled and grated
   fresh ginger

‖ Easy & Delicious Tip ‖

**Seasoning meat with
fruit adds a Korean flair**

   In Korea, fruits like
apples and pears are
often used to flavor meat.
Not only do fruits add a
natural sweetness, but they
also contain enzymes that
tenderize the meat.

 step 1 ## Cut the vegetables

Cut the green onion into 2-in (5-cm) lengths. Cut the garlic chives into 2-in (5-cm) pieces. If using *enoki* mushrooms, cut off the root end and halve the mushrooms crosswise, then separate the slender stalks. If using button mushrooms, slice thinly. Cut the chili pepper diagonally into thin slices.

 step 2 ## Season the meat

Cut the beef into bite-size strips as shown. Combine the ingredients from Ⓐ and stir well. Add to the meat, then mix with your hands.

 step 3 ## Mix the ingredients

 I see! You have to mix in the vegetables *before* frying!

Add the green onion, garlic chives, mushrooms and fresh chili pepper from step 1 to the meat and mix together.

 step 4 ## Stir-fry

【 ◖◖◗ Medium-high heat 】

Heat a frying pan over medium-high heat. Add the mixture from step 3, and stir-fry for 3 to 4 minutes, stirring frequently, until the meat is cooked through.

Ingredient Note

Fresh Chili Peppers: Indispensable for Korean Cooking

Korean chili peppers are slightly sweet, and are often used to garnish meat dishes and to flavor stir-fries. Thai chili peppers are hotter, so use less. Jalapeño peppers are similar in terms of heat, but are much bigger. So adjust the quantity accordingly.

Pot

Total time 15 min

Sundubu-jjigae Soft Tofu Stew with Clams

The savory flavor of dried sardines and Manila clams permeates this spicy soft tofu stew.

[Serves 4]

10 oz (300 g) fresh Manila or steamer clams, in shells

4 green onions (scallions) or baby leeks

6 cups (1.5 liters) Korean-style Fish Stock (see page 19) or 6 teaspoons dashi stock powder with 6 cups (1.5 liters) water

1½ cups (250 g) cabbage kimchi (well-aged, if available)

A 4 tablespoons soy sauce

4 tablespoons Korean red pepper powder or ground red pepper

1 teaspoon minced garlic

1½ lbs (700 g) soft tofu

4 eggs

Easy & Delicious Tip

Soft tofu varieties are interchangeable

Capture the authentic flavor with chunks of soft tofu. Authentic Korean Sundubu-jjigae uses extra-soft tofu (*sundubu*), but it can be easily replaced with soft or silken tofu (*yeondubu*). Tear the soft tofu apart with your hands to get a texture just like the original!

step 1   Remove sand from the clams

Put the clams in a strainer set inside a bowl. Cover with salt water (1 tablespoon salt per 2 cups/500 ml water). Leave in a dark place for 2 to 3 hours to expel sand and grit. Strain, then wash the clams under running water, rubbing the shells together. Discard clams with broken shells or that stay open when tapped smartly.

step 2   Cut the green onions

Cut the white part of the green onions or baby leeks diagonally into thin slices.

step 3   Cook the clams

Combine the sardine stock and the cleaned clams in a pot and bring to a boil over medium heat. Add the kimchi and ingredients from . Cook for 2 to 3 minutes, until the clams open.

【 🌢🌢🌢 Medium heat 】

step 4   Add the tofu

Break the tofu into bite-size chunks by hand and add them to the pot. Then add the green onion from step 2.

【 🌢🌢🌢 Medium heat 】

step 5   Add the eggs

Break the eggs into a bowl and add them to the pot. Simmer for 5 to 6 minutes until cooked to taste.

 You can cook the eggs as firm as you like! If you prefer them runny, just turn off the heat sooner.

【 🌢🌢🌢 Medium heat 】

Saucepan | Frying Pan | Total time 30 min

Japchae Glass Noodles with Fresh Vegetables

This stir-fry is loaded with meat and vegetables and the fragrant aroma of sesame oil and sesame seeds. It's easy to prepare with any type of glass noodles!

[Serves 4]

3½ oz (100 g) dried glass noodles
2 dried wood-ear mushrooms (optional)
½ medium carrot
¼ medium white onion
4 shiitake mushrooms
Small bunch of garlic chives or regular chives
7 oz (200 g) thinly sliced beef
A 1 teaspoon soy sauce
   2 teaspoons sake or cooking sherry
   1 teaspoon minced garlic
2 tablespoons sesame oil
B 2 tablespoons soy sauce
   2 tablespoons *mirin*
¼ teaspoon roasted white sesame seeds
   (See Ingredient Note on page 86)

| Easy & Delicious Tip |

You can substitute chewy Korean glass noodles with Japanese ones

Authentic Japchae is made with thicker, chewy sweet-potato starch noodles called *dangmyeon*. These are called "glass noodles" or "cellophane noodles" in English. If you can't find them, other types of glass noodles can be substituted. I recommend using the springy Japanese glass noodles made from potato starch, rather than the type made from mung bean starch.

【 ◌◌◌ Medium heat 】

Boil the glass noodles

Boil the glass noodles in ample water for about 3 minutes.
Pour into a colander or strainer and drain well.

You can also rehydrate the noodles by soaking them in warm water (about 160°F or 72°C) for 5 minutes, rather than boiling them.

Cut the vegetables

I like to tear wood-ear mushrooms by hand! You can also slice them.

Soak the dried wood-ear mushrooms (if using) in hot water for 20 minutes to rehydrate them, then drain and tear them into small pieces. Cut the carrot and onion into matchsticks. Remove the hard ends from the shiitake mushroom stalks and slice the mushrooms thinly. Cut the garlic chives into 1-in (2.5-cm) lengths.

Season the meat

Slice the meat into thin strips. Combine the marinade ingredients from Ⓐ and mix well, then rub into the meat.

【 ◌◌◌ Medium heat 】　　　【 ◌◌◌ Medium heat 】

Stir-fry

Heat the sesame oil in a frying pan over medium heat. Add the onion and carrot from step 2 and stir-fry until soft. Add the meat from step 3 and cook until the meat is no longer pink, stirring constantly to break the meat apart.

Stir in the shiitake and wood-ear mushrooms prepared in step 2 and continue to fry for 1 minute. Add the glass noodles from step 1 and stir-fry. Mix in the ingredients from Ⓑ, then gently mix in the garlic chives from step 2, stirring well from the bottom of the pan to combine all the ingredients. Transfer to a serving plate and sprinkle the sesame seeds on top.

Frying
Pan

Total time
25 min

┤ Easy & Delicious Tip ├
The secret is in the rice flour!
The key to giving these pancakes
a springy texture is to add
glutinous rice flour (mochi flour) to the
wheat flour in the batter.

Buchimgae Seafood Pancakes

Chewy in the middle, crispy on the outside! A Korean seafood pancake that is truly divine!

[Serves 4]

Small bunch of garlic chives or regular
  chives
3 green onions (scallions)
2 small fresh squid (about 8 oz/225 g)
12 to 16 small fresh shrimp (8 oz/
  225 g total)

Batter

Ⓐ 6 tablespoons all-purpose
    flour
  8 tablespoons glutinous
    rice flour
  ½ teaspoon salt
1½ cups (360 ml) water

4 tablespoons sesame oil, divided
2 eggs, beaten
½ recipe Spicy Dipping Sauce (see
  page 18)

step 1 Prep and cut the vegetables

Cut the chives into 2-in (5-cm) lengths. Chop the white parts of the green onions into small pieces.

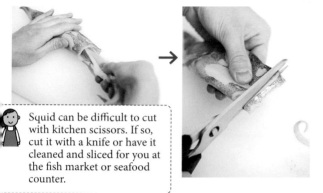

> Squid can be difficult to cut with kitchen scissors. If so, cut it with a knife or have it cleaned and sliced for you at the fish market or seafood counter.

step 2 Cut the squid

Separate the body from the tentacles. Pull out the cartilage, and wash the body. Remove the entrails, eyes and beak from the tentacles, then wash the tentacles. Cut the body into ¼-in (6-mm) rings with kitchen scissors. Cut the tentacles apart in groups of 2 or 3.

step 3 Cut the shrimp

Peel and devein each shrimp using a bamboo skewer, then cut them into 4 small pieces with a knife or kitchen scissors.

step 4 Make the batter

Combine the ingredients from **A** in a bowl. Slowly add the water, stirring constantly to create a smooth batter. Add the garlic chives, green onions, squid and shrimp, then lightly mix them all together.

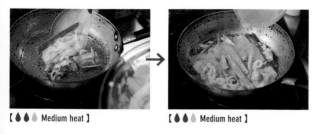

[🔸🔸🔸 Medium heat]   [🔸🔸🔸 Medium heat]

step 5 Cook

Heat 1 tablespoon of the sesame oil in a frying pan over medium heat. Pour ¼ of the batter into the pan. Cook for 2 to 3 minutes, until the edges brown slightly.

Pour ¼ of the beaten egg mixture over the top and cook for another minute. Then turn the pancake over and cook for another 1 to 2 minutes before removing from the heat. Transfer to a plate and repeat with remaining batter. Pour the Spicy Dipping Sauce over the pancakes to serve.

Variations on Buchimgae

Try making different types of *buchimgae* by changing the ingredients and size!

Frying Pan

Total time
20 min

Pork and Pepper Buchimgae Pancakes

Accented with chili peppers for a bit of heat, these round pancakes are smaller, which makes them easy to serve individually.

[Serves 4]

12 oz (340 g) pork loin, thinly sliced
Generous pinch salt and pepper
Ⓐ 1 cup (120 g) all-purpose flour
4 tablespoons potato starch or cornstarch
½ teaspoon salt
1 cup (250 ml) water
5 thin green onions (scallions), finely chopped
2 eggs
2 tablespoons vegetable oil
2 tablespoons sesame oil
1 tablespoon fresh green chili pepper, finely chopped

Dipping Sauce

2 tablespoons soy sauce
2 tablespoons rice vinegar
2 teaspoons sugar

※ This sauce is similar to the one on page 18, but it doesn't include chili pepper.

Cut the pork into thin ¼ in (6 mm) long slices and season with the salt and pepper, mixing to blend.

Combine the ingredients from Ⓐ in a bowl and add the water slowly, stirring constantly to make a smooth batter.

Mix in the seasoned pork and the green onion, then add the eggs. Lightly mix in the eggs so that the yolks are broken apart but not perfectly blended.

Heat 1 tablespoon of each type of oil in a frying pan over medium heat. Pour out half of the batter to make six small round pancakes, and scatter half of the chili pepper over the top. Cook for about 2 minutes, turning the pancakes over when the edges darken, then cook for another 2 minutes until cooked through. Repeat to make all the pancakes.

Blend the Dipping Sauce ingredients and serve with the pancakes in small saucers.

You can cook more or fewer pancakes at a time depending on the size of your pan. Using more oil will make them crunchier.

Clam and Green Onion Buchimgae

Long green onion packed closely together make this pancake look extra appealing!

[Makes 2 large pancakes]

10 thin green onions (scallions)
12 oz (340 g) canned or freshly
    shucked clams
Ⓐ ½ cup (60 g) all-purpose flour
| ½ teaspoon salt
Ⓑ 6 tablespoons glutinous rice
    flour
| 1 cup (250 ml) water

2 tablespoons sesame oil, divided

Dipping Sauce

2 tablespoons finely chopped fresh chili
    peppers
2 tablespoons soy sauce
2 teaspoons sugar
2 teaspoons sesame oil

Cut the green onion into quarters lengthwise. Put the clams in a strainer and immerse in cold water with a pinch of salt (not included in ingredient list). Wash by shaking the clams, then dry them on paper towels. Divide the clams and green onions into two equal parts.

Combine the Ⓐ ingredients in a bowl. Blend together the Ⓑ ingredients, then slowly add them to Ⓐ, mixing continuously until combined.

Heat 1 tablespoon of the sesame oil in a frying pan over medium heat. Lay ½ of the prepared clams and green onions in the pan, and then pour ½ of the batter over to cover. Reduce heat to medium-low and cook for 2–3 minutes. Flip when the edges darken, and cook about 3 more minutes until cooked through. Repeat to make a second pancake.

Combine the Dipping Sauce ingredients and mix well. Cut the pancakes into bite-size pieces and transfer to a serving plate. Serve the sauce alongside.

TIP

Lay the ingredients in the pan before covering them with the batter

If you pour the batter in after arranging the green onions and clams in the pan, the pancake will look beautiful and the ingredients will be evenly distributed.

Frying Pan

Total time
25 min

Saucepan Frying Pan Total time 30 min

※ Not including marinating time

Samgyeopsal Grilled Pork Belly

Samgyeopsal is a crispy grilled pork dish that translates to "three-layered meat."
Wrap it in a leaf of lettuce or another fresh, mild green and dig in!

[Serves 4]

2 lbs (1 kg) sliced pork belly
Ⓐ 1 cup (250 ml) dry white wine
2 cloves garlic, thinly sliced
1½ teaspoons salt

6 cabbage leaves
2 fresh chili peppers (1 green, 1 red)
1 head red-leaf lettuce
Ⓑ 4 tablespoons sesame oil
1 teaspoon salt

2 cloves garlic, thinly sliced
16 green perilla leaves
   (or shiso leaves)
Green Onion Salad (see opposite)
Gochujang red chili bean paste, to serve

Cut and marinate the meat

Slice the meat lengthwise into six rashers and place in a plastic bag. Mix together the ingredients from **A**, pour over the meat, and mix to coat well. Place in the refrigerator for 1–4 hours so the flavors can mingle.

Prepare the vegetables

Cut each cabbage leaf into 3 equal parts. Quickly blanch in boiling water, then cool in a strainer. Cut the chili peppers diagonally into thin slices. Wash and dry the lettuce. Mix together the sesame oil and salt from **B**.

Replicate the flavors of a specialty restaurant with this simple Green Onion Salad!

Samgyeopsal is always accompanied by green onion salad, so try making this garnish at home. Cut 16 green onions into very thin matchsticks and rinse with cold water, then pat gently to remove all moisture. Mix together 1 teaspoon red chili pepper flakes with seeds (or ½ teaspoon milder pepper flakes without seeds), 2 teaspoons sesame oil and ½ teaspoon salt. Pour over the green onions and stir well.

Grill the meat

【 Medium heat 】

Heat a frying pan over medium heat. Remove the pork from the marinade and blot away any excess liquid, then lay the slices on the pan to cook. Add the garlic and cook together. Drain off the grease coming out of the meat or wipe away with a paper towel. Cook for 3–4 minutes until browned.

Turn the pork over and cook for another 1–2 minutes, then cut into bite-size pieces with kitchen scissors and cook a little longer.

 The trick to getting a crispy texture is to grill both sides of the pork, then cut it into smaller pieces and quickly grill it again.

 For the wraps, I highly recommend cabbage as well as lettuce. You can add your other favorite vegetables, and enjoy them along with the chili pepper and garlic in a mouth-watering Samgyeopsal!

Wrap the meat in leafy greens

To serve, place a piece of cooked pork on a cabbage, lettuce or perilla leaf. Wrap it up with some fried garlic, chili pepper and/or Green Onion Salad and top with the mixed **B** ingredients as a sauce.

Hearty Pork and Potato Stew

Cook whole potatoes and spare ribs together in this hearty stew.

[Serves 4]

12 pork spare ribs
6 green perilla leaves
    (or shiso leaves)
4 green onions (scallions)
2 tablespoons ground white
    sesame seeds
8 small potatoes (2 lbs/1 kg)
4 teaspoons beef bouillon powder
8 cups (2 liters) water

Ⓐ 4 tablespoons *gochujang* red
    chili bean paste
2 tablespoons Korean red pepper
    powder or ground red pepper
    (see page 14)
2 teaspoons sesame oil
1 teaspoon minced garlic

┃ Easy & Delicious Tip ┃

Japanese green shiso leaves and Vietnamese perilla have almost the same taste as Korean green perilla leaves

Green perilla leaves are often used in Korean cooking (see page 15). Shiso leaves, another variety of perilla, have a similar flavor, so you can easily use them as a substitute for the Korean variety.

Classic
Korean Dish
7

Pot

Total time
60 min

step 1 Blanch the meat

Quickly blanch the spare ribs in a few cups of boiling water until the outside of the meat turns white. Immerse in cool water and wipe off any foam or grease.

 ### step 2 Prep the vegetables

Cut the perilla leaves into sixths, cut the white parts of the green onions diagonally into thin slices, and mix together with the ground sesame seeds. Peel the potatoes and cut into halves or quarters.

 ### step 3 Begin cooking the stew

Place the meat from step 1, the bouillon powder and the water in a large pot over medium heat. Bring to a boil and cook for about 15 minutes, then add the ingredients from **A** and stir well.

【 ◗◗◗◗ Medium heat 】

 ### step 4 Add the potatoes

Add the potatoes from step 2 and cook for about 15 minutes. When the potatoes are tender, add the vegetables from step 2, stir, and enjoy!

【 ◗◗◗◗ Medium heat 】

Dak-galbi Chicken with Spicy Garlic Sauce

The sweet and spicy sauce in this dish makes it difficult to resist! The large portion sizes of this chicken and vegetable stir-fry are sure to satisfy.

[Serves 4]

Ⓐ 4 tablespoons *gochujang* red chili bean paste
  2 tablespoons sake or rice wine
  2 tablespoons sesame oil
  1 tablespoon soy sauce
  1 tablespoon sugar
  1 teaspoon peeled and grated fresh ginger
  1 tablespoon minced garlic
1½ lbs (700 g) boneless chicken thigh meat
1¼ lbs (600 g) cabbage

6 green onions (scallions)
1 white onion
½ carrot
1 or 2 sweet potatoes (14 oz/400 g)
1 tablespoon sesame oil
1 cup (250 ml) water

┤ Easy & Delicious Tip ├

Don't worry if sauce sticks to the pan. Just wipe it away!

This sweet and spicy sauce burns easily, so take care when stir-frying. If the sauce does begin sticking to the pan, use a wet paper towel between two chopsticks to wipe away the burnt bits.

Classic Korean Dish 8

Frying Pan

Total time
30 min

※ Not including marinating time

step 1 Season the meat

Mix the ingredients from Ⓐ together in a bowl. Cut the chicken into bite-size pieces, then add them to the bowl with mixture Ⓐ. Rub the seasoning into the meat by hand. Let it sit for about 10 minutes.

> Adding the seasoning before cooking ensures that the meat is flavorful all through.

step 2 Prepare the vegetables

> Soaking the cut sweet potatoes in cool water can prevent a bitter taste. Change the water whenever it starts turning cloudy until it finally stays clear.

Cut the cabbage into small strips, and slice the white parts of the green onions diagonally into thin slices.

Cut the onion into very thin slices. Cut the carrot into thin strips. Peel the sweet potato and cut it into thin matchsticks. Soak the cut sweet potato in cool water and drain just before using.

【 🌢🌢🌢 Medium heat 】

【 🌢🌢🌢 Medium heat 】

step 3 Stir-fry and Steam

Heat the sesame oil in a frying pan over medium heat. Add the chicken from step 1 along with all the marinade. Stir-fry for about 2 minutes, making sure the sauce doesn't burn. Add the onion, carrot and drained sweet potato, and stir-fry for about another 2 minutes.

Add the cabbage, green onion and water, and cover the pan with a lid. Let it simmer over medium heat for 2 to 3 minutes.

step 4 Finish stir-frying

Remove the lid and stir-fry the ingredients together over medium heat, stirring everything together thoroughly.

> Serve this dish piping-hot right in the pan at the table!

【 🌢🌢🌢 Medium heat 】

Stir-fried Dak-galbi Chicken with Cheese

Cover your Dak-galbi in melted cheese! This style is very popular in Korea now, and you can easily make it at home!

[Serves 4]

1 recipe Dak-galbi (see pages 40–41), divided

½ to ¾ cup (60 to 75 g) grated pizza cheese (mozzarella or provolone)

| Easy & Delicious Tip |

Use a tabletop burner to keep the cheese warm

Once you shut off the heat, the melted cheese will soon begin to harden and the dish will become less appetizing. I recommend keeping the pan warm over a portable burner on the table and serve the melty Dak-galbi right out of the pan like a fondue!

Classic Korean Dish 9

Frying Pan

Total time
35 min

✳ Not including marinating time

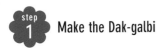

step 1 — Make the Dak-galbi

Make the Dak-galbi in the frying pan by following the recipe on page 41 and remove ⅓ of it to serve as-is. Push the remaining ⅔ to one side of the pan, put the cheese in the empty side of the pan and place over medium heat.

step 2 — Add the finishing touch

When the cheese is melted, lower the heat and mix everything together to serve.

【 ◌◌◌ Medium heat 】

【 ◌◌◌ Low heat 】

You can enjoy two different tastes by eating a third of the Dak-galbi recipe (pages 40–41) as-is, and by adding cheese to the rest.

Tip — More to enjoy! A touch of creativity

The last stop for leftover Dak-galbi is to turn it into Dak-galbi Fried Rice!

Waste not! Instead of throwing away your leftover Dak-galbi, make it into fried rice like they do in Korea.

Ingredients and directions

For about ¼ of a recipe of Dak-galbi: Cut the leftover chicken into small bite-size pieces with kitchen scissors; tear up a sheet of *nori* seaweed. Heat 2 teaspoons of sesame oil in a frying pan. Add 2 cups (400 g) of cooked white rice, the chicken and the *nori*. Stir-fry together over medium heat for 3 minutes. Level the surface of the rice and leave over low heat for 1 to 2 minutes. The rice is especially tasty when it gets a little crispy on the bottom.

Pot

Total time
25 min

Yukgaejang Spicy Beef Soup

This is a spicy soup with a rich beef base. It can boost your stamina too,
so I recommend this dish when you're feeling low on energy!

[Serves 4]

4 cups (125 g) fresh spinach
2 cups (200 g) bean sprouts
4 shiitake mushrooms
½ cup (75 g) boiled Asian royal
fern (optional, see sidebar,
opposite)
12 oz (350 g) beef, thinly sliced

2 tablespoons sesame oil
2 cloves garlic, finely chopped
2 tablespoons peeled fresh ginger,
finely chopped
Ⓐ 6 cups (1.5 liters) water
4 teaspoons beef stock powder
Ⓑ 4 tablespoons *gochujang* red
chili bean paste

2 teaspoons Korean red pepper
powder or ground red pepper
2 tablespoons soy sauce
2 tablespoons *mirin*

 Prepared beef stock can be
used instead of the water
and beef stock powder!

step 1 — Cut the vegetables

Slice the spinach into large pieces. Remove the roots from the bean sprouts. Remove the hard ends from the shiitake mushroom stalks and slice the mushrooms thinly. Cut the fern into bite-size lengths, if using.

step 2 — Cut the meat

Cut the meat into bite-size strips.

step 3 — Stir-fry and simmer

Heat the sesame oil in a pot. Add the garlic, ginger and vegetables from step 1 and the meat from step 2 and quickly stir-fry over medium heat. Pour in the ingredients from **Ⓐ**. Bring the liquid to a boil and skim any foam off the top. Add the ingredients from **Ⓑ** and cook for 1 to 2 minutes more before serving.

【 🌢🌢🌢 Medium heat 】

Ingredient Note

Already familiar from the recipe for Bibimbap, this wild plant makes an appearance in many traditional Korean dishes. You can substitute turnip or mushrooms instead.

Asian Royal Fern

This edible wild plant is frequently used in recipes like soups and *namul* for Bibimbap (see page 24). It is characterized by its spiral-tipped stalks. If you can buy the ferns boiled, it will save you time. If you are boiling the fern yourself, there are ways to reduce its bitterness. One way is to combine 4 cups (1 liter) water, 4 tablespoons wheat flour and 2 teaspoons salt in a pot, bring the mixture to a boil, and boil the fern pieces for about 3 minutes. Transfer the fern to a bowl of cold water and let stand for about 10 minutes, and it's ready to use!

Classic
Korean Dish
11

Saucepan　Frying Pan　Total time 25 min

Stir-fried Tteok-bokki Rice Cakes

These rice cakes coated with a sweet and spicy sauce are addictive! This traditional dish is normally sold in Korean food stands but now you can enjoy it at home!

[Serves 4]

14 oz (400 g) tube-shaped rice cakes (*tteok*, see page 17)

4 hard-boiled eggs

Ⓐ 4 tablespoons *gochujang* red chili bean paste

1 tablespoon sugar

2 teaspoons soy sauce

½ white onion

½ carrot

6 Vienna sausages or mini hot dogs

4 Japanese or Thai fried fish cakes

2 teaspoons sesame oil

1 cup (250 ml) water

┤ Easy & Delicious Tip ├

Pre-boiling is a shortcut to making delicious rice cakes

Partially cook the rice cakes by boiling first as indicated in step 1 so that they will quickly become soft after stir-frying in step 3 and step 4. If you can't get cylindrical *tteok* rice cakes, you can slice a block of Japanese *kirimochi* rice cake into bars instead.

 step 1 Blanch the rice cakes

Bring water to a boil in a saucepan, then add the cylindrical rice cakes. When the water returns to a boil, remove from the heat and pour into a strainer. Peel the boiled eggs. Combine the sauce ingredients in **A** and mix well.

step 2 Cut the ingredients

Slice the onion into ¼ in (6 mm) half-moons. Cut the carrot into thin sticks about 2 in (5 cm) long and ½ in (1.25 cm) wide. Cut the sausages into small diagonal pieces. Slice the fish cake into bite-size pieces.

 step 3 Stir-fry

Heat the sesame oil in a frying pan over medium heat. Add the onion, carrot, sausage and fishcake from step 2. Stir-fry until the onion becomes transparent, then add the rice cakes from step 1 and sauté all together.

【 🌢🌢🌢 Medium heat 】

Ingredient Note

Korea's beloved stick-shaped rice cakes

Rice Cakes for Tteok-bokki

The rice cakes used in Tteok-bokki are 1½–2 in (3.75–5 cm) long cylinders. In Korean, *tteok* means "rice cake" and *bokki* means "stir-fry." Korean rice cakes hold together well, making them ideally suited for dishes like Tteok-bokki that are stir-fried and then simmered.

 step 4 Simmer

When everything is well mixed, add in **A** and 1 cup of water and stir. Add the boiled eggs and simmer over medium heat for about 2 to 3 minutes, or until only a third of the broth remains. Serve hot with rice.

【 🌢🌢🌢 Medium heat 】

Easy & Delicious Tip
Use your hands to mix in the seasonings!

When you dress the vegetables with the *namul* seasoning, try using your hands to mix them together. This helps the flavors mingle so the vegetables become even more delicious (see page 101).

Saucepan Frying Pan Total time 25 min

Three-color Namul Salad

Namul refers to any type of seasoned vegetable preparation. It may describe a variety of vegetables, but for now, let's learn to prepare three basic types.

[Serves 4]

2 cups (200 g) bean sprouts
2 teaspoons sesame oil, divided
Ⓐ 2 tablespoons sake or cooking sherry
   ½ teaspoon chicken soup powder
1 large carrot
8 oz (225 g) fresh spinach
½ teaspoon soy sauce

Namul Seasoning

(This *namul* seasoning recipe is enough to flavor one vegetable. If you are making all 3 vegetables, triple the quantities in Ⓑ).

Ⓑ ½ teaspoon salt
   ¼ teaspoon minced garlic
   2 tablespoons ground white sesame seeds

Removing the roots and husks from the bean sprouts gives them a more appealing texture.

【 ◊◊◊ Medium heat 】

step 1 Prepare the bean sprouts Namul

Remove the roots and husks from the bean sprouts. Heat 1 teaspoon of the sesame oil in a frying pan over medium heat, then add the sprouts and Seasoning ingredients from Ⓐ and stir-fry for 2 to 3 minutes until the sprouts are tender. Add the ingredients from Ⓑ and stir-fry everything together.

【 ◊◊◊ Medium heat 】

step 2 Prepare the carrot Namul

Peel the carrot and use a mandoline or large box grater to slice it into fine shreds. Heat the remaining 1 teaspoon of the sesame oil in a frying pan over medium heat, then add and stir-fry the carrot. Once tender, add the Seasoning ingredients from Ⓑ and stir-fry everything together.

【 ◊◊◊ Medium heat 】 【 ◊◊◊ Medium heat 】

step 3 Prepare the spinach Namul

Wash the spinach leaves well to remove any grit. Fill a saucepan with water and add a pinch of salt (not included in the ingredients list). Bring to a boil. Add the spinach and quickly blanch, then plunge in cold water to stop the cooking. Strain and firmly squeeze out any remaining liquid. Cut the spinach into 2-in (5-cm) pieces, sprinkle the soy sauce over it, and squeeze again. Dress with the Seasoning from Ⓑ just before serving.

Tip More to enjoy! A touch of creativity

Remember the basic ingredients in Namul seasoning for a delicious way to use up leftover vegetables!

The style of cooking known as *namul* suits almost any type of vegetable and there is a saying, "There are as many types of *namul* as there are vegetables." Sesame oil, minced garlic and salt form the foundation of the flavor. From there, you can add other ingredients like sesame seeds, sugar and soy sauce to suit each type of vegetable. If you add these basic seasonings, even vegetables that were previously uneaten can become a popular dish!

No cooking required

Total time	Storage
20 min	3~4 days

Quick Napa Cabbage Kimchi

Delicious even without any special ingredients! This easy,
lightly pickled kimchi can be eaten the same day it's made.

[Serves 4]

¼ to ½ head napa cabbage
   (about 1 lb/450 g)
Small bunch garlic chives
4 thin green onions (scallions)
½ teaspoon sea salt

Ⓐ 2 tablespoons grated apple or pear
   1 teaspoon minced garlic
   1 teaspoon peeled and grated fresh
      ginger
   1 teaspoon salt
   1 teaspoon sugar
   2 teaspoons fish sauce
   2 teaspoons sesame oil
3 tablespoons Korean red chili pepper
   powder or ground red pepper (see
   page 14)

These are all the seasonings
you'll need. All of these
can be bought at most
supermarkets.

step 1 · Cut the vegetables

Separate the leaves of the napa cabbage. Slice the leaves diagonally to make thick pieces. Cut the garlic chives and green onions into 1-in (2.5-cm) lengths.

step 2 · Salt the vegetables

Place the napa cabbage, garlic chives and green onions in a food storage bag. Mix in the salt well with your hand and let sit for about 15 minutes or until the vegetables become soft. Lightly press the vegetables from outside of the bag to squeeze out the water, then discard it.

step 3 · Dress the vegetables

Add the ingredients from **A** and evenly coat all the vegetables by lightly working it through the vegetables from outside of the bag. You can eat this kimchi right away, but if you let it sit in the refrigerator for an hour or more, the flavors will mingle and become even more delicious.

 This kimchi will keep inside the bag in the refrigerator for 3 to 4 days.

Re-create the authentic taste of kimchi made with salted fermented shrimp by using Thai or Vietnamese fish sauce

Ingredient Note

Thai Fish Sauce (*nam pla*)

Kimchi is traditionally made with tiny salted fermented shrimp, but Thai or Vietnamese fish sauce is easier to obtain and can be used as a substitute. This condiment, which is made from the clear liquid that comes out when sardines are fermented in saltwater, is available in most supermarkets. It has a unique savory tang and saltiness.

No cooking required

Total time	Storage
12 min	3~4 days

Quick Cucumber Kimchi

A delightfully crunchy cucumber kimchi. Just add seasoned daikon radish and carrots!

[Serves 4]

4 Japanese cucumbers or pickling
   gherkins
½ teaspoon salt
1 small daikon radish (7 oz/200 g)
½ carrot
Ⓐ 2 tablespoons grated apple
1 teaspoon minced garlic

1 teaspoon peeled and grated fresh ginger
1 teaspoon salt
1 teaspoon sugar
2 teaspoons fish sauce
2 teaspoons sesame oil
3 tablespoons Korean red chili pepper
   powder or ground red pepper
   (see page 14)

The seasoning used for this is the same as the seasoning for Quick Napa Cabbage Kimchi on pages 50–51!

step 1 Prepare the cucumbers

Cut the cucumbers at diagonal angles into large chunks of about equal size. Put the chunks into a food storage bag, add the salt and let sit for about 10 minutes. Lightly press the cucumber from outside of the bag to squeeze out the water, then discard it.

step 2 Prepare the daikon and carrot

Use a mandoline or large box grater to shred the daikon radish and carrot into fine threads. Place in a bowl and mix in the ingredients from Ⓐ.

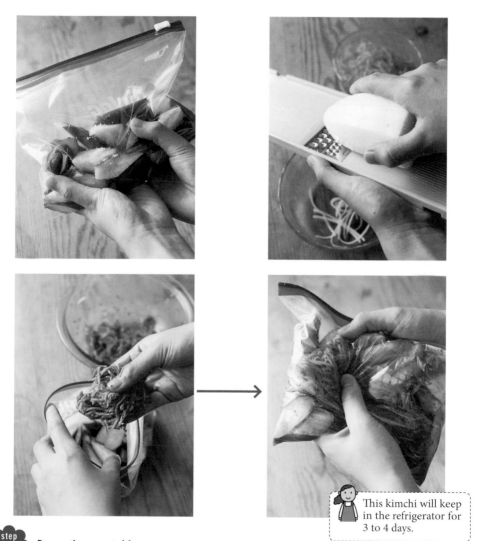

This kimchi will keep in the refrigerator for 3 to 4 days.

step 3 Dress the vegetables

Add the daikon and carrot mixture to the bag of cucumber and evenly dress all the vegetables by lightly massaging them from outside of the bag. You can eat the kimchi right away, but if you let it sit in the refrigerator for an hour the flavors will mingle and become even tastier.

Chapter 2

These Korean main dishes are all very quick and easy to prepare!

Let the irresistible flavors of Korean food take center stage in your everyday meals.

Meat and Fish Dishes

In Korea, steaming hot white rice is a dietary staple. The following meat and fish recipes will perfectly complement white rice, in addition to having generous portion sizes, giving you healthy energy, and requiring little cooking time. Combine everyday ingredients with new seasonings and cooking styles to create fresh tastes! As you try more variations, your cooking knowledge will really grow.

TIPS

Get a crisp texture by using the right amount of frying oil!

Add enough oil to cover ½ to ⅔ the thickness of the chicken, and fry it on both sides to get it crispy. If the temperature is right, there should be large bubbles rising up through the oil.

Evenly coat the fried chicken pieces with the sauce

Thoroughly coat the outside of the fried chicken by dredging each piece in the sauce.

Korean Fried Chicken

Add Korean flair to fried chicken with a sweet and spicy *gochujang* sauce! This dish is a huge hit with my family!

[Serves 4]

1½ lbs (700 g) boneless chicken thighs
A 2 eggs
2 tablespoons flour
2 tablespoons sake or cooking sherry
4 tablespoons potato starch or cornstarch
½ teaspoon salt
½ teaspoon freshly ground black pepper
B 4 tablespoons *gochujang* red chili bean paste
2 tablespoons honey
2 teaspoons soy sauce
1 teaspoon minced garlic
1 teaspoon peeled and grated fresh ginger
Cooking oil, as needed for deep-frying
⅓ cup (40 g) chopped roasted peanuts, to garnish (optional)

Cut the chicken into large bite-size pieces. Blend the ingredients from **A** together in a bowl and add the chicken pieces.

Combine the ingredients from **B** in a separate bowl.

In a heavy, deep frying pan, heat about 1 in (2.5 cm) of cooking oil to 340°F (170°C) and add the chicken coated with the ingredients from **A**. Let it fry for about 1 minute, then turn it over and fry for another 3 minutes, occasionally turning the chicken over again and stirring. Finally, slightly raise the heat and fry for about 30 seconds more until very crispy (but do not burn). Transfer to a rack or paper towel-covered plate to drain.

Coat the chicken pieces with the **B** mixture while it is still hot, then arrange on a serving plate. Sprinkle the chopped peanuts over the top, if using.

Frying Pan

Total time
20 min

Raising the heat slightly for the last 30 seconds of frying makes the chicken really crispy!

 TIPS

Pound the roughly chopped meat with your knife to make it stick together

Adding larger pieces of coarsely chopped beef to the ground beef or pork changes the texture and makes the patties taste better. If you pound the beef with your knife after you chop it up, it will become slightly sticky and easier to form into a patty.

Grill the patties for a better flavor

On a grill, extra grease falls away and the meat makes a nice savory smell as it cooks, so this method is superior to pan frying although you can do that also to save time. You can make the patties thinner if you wish to have them well-done.

Galbi Short-rib Patties

These fragrant grilled Korean beef patties are wonderfully easy to make!

[Serves 4]

1 lb (450 g) beef, thinly sliced
8 oz (225 g) ground beef or pork (or a mixture)
4 green onions (scallions), white parts only,
    chopped
Ⓐ 2 tablespoons soy sauce
    2 tablespoons sake or cooking sherry
    2 tablespoons sugar
    1 tablespoon sesame oil
    1 teaspoon minced garlic
    2 tablespoons finely chopped fresh chili
        peppers (you can substitute ½ teaspoon
        dried red chili flakes although fresh chilies
        are more fragrant)
    ¼ teaspoon salt
    ¼ teaspoon freshly ground black pepper
Leafy vegetables like green-leaf and red-leaf
    lettuce, and perilla leaves, as desired
Fresh garlic chives and *gochujang*, to serve
    (optional)

Coarsely mince the sliced beef with a large knife or cleaver, then pound it with the back of a knife until it becomes sticky. Combine the beef with the ground meat and the chopped green onions in a bowl. Mix the ingredients from Ⓐ separately until well blended, then add to the meat and knead everything together.

Lay aluminum foil on a grill pan. Divide the meat mixture into eight equal parts and shape into flat, circular or square patties. Broil on the foil under high heat for about 2 minutes, or until the meat browns, then lower the heat to medium and cook for 2 more minutes. Flip the patties and grill for 2 to 3 more minutes until cooked through.

Transfer to a serving plate and enjoy with leafy vegetables.

Small Grill	Total time
	20 min

Galbi Patties are also tasty if you tear them into small pieces and wrap them in leafy vegetables. For more flavor, garnish the wraps with *gochujang* red chili bean paste, kimchi, raw garlic slices, Spicy Dipping Sauce (see page 18), and the like.

How to enjoy this dish

Lay a perilla leaf on a blanched cabbage leaf and add a slice of pork, kimchi, salted fermented shrimp and a dollop of the miso-*mirin* sauce. The savoriness of the cabbage and the saltiness of the fermented shrimp and miso-*mirin* sauce give the pork an authentic Korean taste.

Simmered Pork Belly

Wrap this moist, tender boiled pork up in pickled cabbage to complement the rich taste of the meat.

[Serves 4]

1½ lbs (700 g) pork belly
1 knob fresh ginger, peeled and coarsely chopped
4 green onions (scallions), white parts only, coarsely chopped
1 small daikon radish (7 oz/200 g), peeled
½ teaspoon salt
One bunch chives, chopped
Ⓐ 2 teaspoons *gochujang* red chili bean paste
| 1 teaspoon sugar
| 1 teaspoon rice vinegar
Ⓑ 4 tablespoons miso
| 4 tablespoons *mirin*
| 1 teaspoon minced garlic
½ head napa cabbage
20 Korean perilla leaves (or shiso leaves)
1½ cups (250 g) sliced kimchi
6 tablespoons salted fermented shrimp
Gochujang red chili bean paste, to serve

Bring 3 quarts (3 liters) of water to a boil in a large pot. Add the pork, ginger and green onion, and simmer for 30 to 40 minutes over low heat. When the juices run clear when meat is pierced, remove from heat. Leave the meat in the broth until it cools.

Cut the daikon into rods about ¼ in (6 mm) wide, sprinkle with the salt, and let stand for 15 minutes. Cut the chives into ½ in (1.25 cm) long pieces. Just before serving, firmly squeeze the moisture from the daikon. Combine the ingredients from **Ⓐ**, add the daikon and chives, and toss to blend well.

Mix the ingredients from **Ⓑ** in a microwave-safe container, cover with plastic wrap, and heat in the microwave for about 30 seconds.

Bring a large pot of water to a boil over high heat. Add 2 tablespoons of salt. Peel off individual cabbage leaves and blanch several of them at a time for 2–3 minutes per batch, until the leaves have softened slightly. Use a slotted spoon to transfer the leaves to an ice bath. Once the leaves are cool, drain them well on a paper towel-lined plate or in a colander.

Remove the pork from the broth and slice it into bite-size chunks as shown in the photo. Serve it alongside the seasoned daikon and chive, the miso-*mirin* sauce, the perilla leaves, the kimchi and the salted fermented shrimp.

Pot	Microwave	Total time
		45 min

TIP

Let the simmered pork cool in its broth

If you let the meat cool down in the broth, the pork will stay moist instead of becoming dry and tough.

Frying Pan with Lid

Total time
40 min

⁂ Not including the time to soak the meat

Kimchi Simmered Spare Ribs

These hearty spare ribs, simmered under a layer of kimchi, are packed with flavor!

[Serves 4]

12 pork spare ribs, about 2 lbs (1 kg) total

Ⓐ 2 cups (500 ml) water
½ cup (125 ml) sake or cooking sherry
2 tablespoons soy sauce

1½ lbs (600 g) napa cabbage kimchi (well-aged with large leaves, if available)

Soak the spare ribs in water for a few minutes to remove the blood. Drain well and pat the meat dry.

Arrange the ribs in a deep frying pan, pour in the ingredients from Ⓐ, then lay the kimchi leaves over the meat to cover.

Cover the pan with a lid. Bring to a boil over high heat, then cook at medium-low heat for 30 minutes, simmering until the liquid is reduced by half or more. Check occasionally to see that the liquid is not completely gone, and add more if needed.

Cut the kimchi into bite-size pieces with kitchen scissors or a knife, and serve alongside the spare ribs.

If you can't find whole-leaf kimchi, you can use sliced kimchi, but reduce the quantity slightly. Check the taste partway through cooking, and add a bit more kimchi if necessary.

TIP

Spread the kimchi on top of the meat

When you place the kimchi over the spare ribs, spread the leaves out so that they cover the meat. This allows the flavors of the kimchi to permeate the ribs completely.

Braised Spicy Pork and Vegetables

It's easy to make the same sweet and spicy vegetable and meat dish that you enjoy at Korean restaurants.

[Serves 4]

1 small white onion
1 medium carrot
1 small zucchini
1 green bell pepper
Ⓐ 1½ cups (360 ml) water
    4 tablespoons *gochujang* red chili bean paste
    1 tablespoon soy sauce
    1 tablespoon sugar
    1 teaspoon minced garlic
    1 teaspoon peeled and grated fresh ginger
1 lb (450 g) pork, thinly sliced
1 teaspoon sesame oil (or more, to taste)

Peel and halve the onion, carrot and zucchini lengthwise and slice them into ⅛ in (3 mm) thick half-moons. Quarter the bell pepper lengthwise and slice it into ¼-in (6-mm) strips.

Combine the ingredients from Ⓐ in the frying pan, then add the pork and bring to a boil over medium heat. Skim off any foam that appears, then cover with a lid, lower the heat to medium-low and simmer for about 3 minutes.

Remove the lid and add the vegetables. Raise the heat to medium and cook, stirring, for 2 to 3 minutes. Let the liquid evaporate so the dish resembles a stir-fry. When the vegetables are tender, add the sesame oil, remove from the heat and serve.

TIP

Add the vegetables when there is only a bit of liquid remaining

Add the vegetables when there is only a small amount of liquid remaining. Move the liquid around the pan to facilitate evaporation and coat the ingredients well with the concentrated seasonings.

Frying Pan

Total time
25 min

Grilled Beef Short Ribs

Marinate the meat for authentic flavor. Wrap the beef and kimchi in lettuce and dig in!

[Serves 4]

Ⓐ 1 tablespoon soy sauce
1 tablespoon *mirin*
1 teaspoon minced garlic
1 teaspoon peeled and grated fresh ginger
1 teaspoon sesame oil
1 teaspoon ground white sesame seeds

Generous pinch of salt
2 tablespoons grated apple or pear
2 lbs (1 kg) boneless beef short ribs, thinly sliced
1 head red or green leaf lettuce
1½ cups (250 g) kimchi
Seasoned nori (*gim*), to serve

Combine the ingredients from Ⓐ in a bowl. Add the sliced beef and thoroughly rub in the marinade. Allow to marinate for 15 minutes or longer.

Separate the lettuce leaves, wash and dry them individually.

Heat a frying pan over high heat, then sear the marinated beef on both sides until browned.

Serve with kimchi, lettuce leaves and seasoned nori. Wrap each piece of meat with kimchi in the lettuce or nori while it's still hot and eat immediately.

As the beef cooks the fat renders, releasing its aroma. Wrapping the meat up with kimchi in leafy green vegetables is a traditionally light way to enjoy Korean barbeque.

TIP

Massage the marinade ingredients into the meat

When seasoning the beef, thoroughly rub in the sauce by hand. This makes for tender meat and maximum flavor!

Frying Pan

Total time
10 min

※ Not including marinating time

Grilled Beef Rolls

Try preparing your grilled beef as a roll! The thin green onion and shiso leaves add a refreshing flavor to the rich beef.

[Serves 4]

24 thin green onions (scallions)
12 green shiso leaves
2 lbs (1 kg) beef shank (or other thinly sliced beef) cut into 24 flat strips

2 teaspoons vegetable oil
Super Tasty Sauce or Spicy Bean Paste Sauce (page 18), for serving

Cut the green onions into 2-in (5-cm) lengths and cut the shiso leaves in half. Divide the leaves into 24 equal portions.

Wrap each of the individual green onion and shiso leaf portions in a slice of beef as shown below.

Heat the oil in a frying pan over medium-high heat. Place the wraps in the pan seam-side down and cook for 2–3 minutes. Turn the wraps over and cook 2–3 minutes more until browned on all sides. Serve with dipping sauces and rice.

This style of wrap is popular in Korea. Fragrant vegetables like chives, baby leeks and Korean perilla leaves can be wrapped in the same way. If you see them at the supermarket, try it!

TIP

Aim for tidy rolls, but don't worry if they aren't

Even if you don't wrap the vegetables very tightly, the meat will naturally shrink when cooking, creating neater bundles. Place the rolls seam-side down in the pan to start cooking them, to seal the edges together.

Frying Pan

Total time
15 min

※ Not including time for the sauce

Chicken Jjimdak Stew with Vegetables and Noodles

A hearty stew with chicken, potatoes, carrots and glass noodles.

[Serves 4]

4 potatoes, peeled
2 carrots, peeled
½ onion, peeled
2 lbs (900 g) bone-in chicken thighs
1½ cups (350 ml) water
3 oz (75 g) dry glass noodles
1 fresh red chili pepper
🅐 4 tablespoons soy sauce
  4 tablespoons *mirin*
  1 teaspoon minced garlic

Slice the potatoes into rounds. Cut the carrots into thirds lengthwise, then quarter the pieces crosswise. Cut the onion into thin wedges. Cut the chicken thighs into thirds with a cleaver or heavy knife.

Bring water to a boil in a deep frying pan, then add the chicken and vegetables. When it returns to a boil, cover and simmer over low heat for 8 to 10 minutes.

Rehydrate the glass noodles by soaking them in warm water for about 5 minutes. Drain well.

Cut the chili pepper diagonally into thin slices. Add the ingredients from 🅐, the rehydrated noodles and the chili pepper to the pan and raise the heat to medium. Continue to simmer for a few minutes, stirring constantly until the meat and vegetables are cooked and the flavors are well combined.

Deep Frying Pan

Total time
30 min

TIP

Add the seasonings after the chicken and vegetables cook

First, let the chicken and vegetables simmer together. One trick to getting a delicious Jjimdak is allowing the vegetables to soak up the chicken stock—add the seasonings and glass noodles afterwards.

Sliced Pork Belly Stir-fried with Kimchi

Spicy kimchi is a perfect match for pork. Eat this dish with raw tofu and white rice, like they do in Korea—a wonderful combination of flavors and textures!

[Serves 4]

10 oz (300 g) pork belly, thinly sliced
½ teaspoon salt
½ teaspoon freshly ground black pepper
1½ cups (250 g) cabbage kimchi (well-aged, if available)

4 green onions (scallions), white parts only
1 block firm tofu (10 oz/300 g)
2 teaspoons sesame oil
2 teaspoons soy sauce

Frying Pan

Total time 20 min

Slice the pork into thin bite-size pieces. Rub the salt and pepper into the meat. Cut the kimchi into bite-size pieces. Cut the white parts of the green onions diagonally into thin slices. Cut the tofu into ½-in (1.25-cm) cubes.

Heat the sesame oil in a frying pan over medium heat. Add the pork and stir-fry it.

When the meat has browned, drain off most of the grease, leaving only about a table-spoon. Add and quickly stir-fry the sliced onion and kimchi, and then mix in the soy sauce.

Transfer to a platter and serve with the sliced tofu and steaming white rice.

TIP

Remove most of the pork oil after frying to make the dish less greasy!

A lot of oil comes out when you fry the pork. If you drain off the extra grease before adding the vegetables, the dish will have a lighter flavor.

Frying Pan

Total time
35 min

Pork and Kimchi Pot Stickers with Tofu

The savory tang of kimchi is simply addictive! Tofu is added for a more healthy filling.

[Makes 48 pot stickers)

1½ cups (250 g) cabbage kimchi
  (well-aged, if available)
Small bunch garlic chives
10 oz (300 g) firm tofu
14 oz (400 g) ground pork
🅐 2 teaspoons soy sauce
  2 teaspoons sesame oil
  ½ teaspoon salt
  ¼ teaspoon freshly ground
    black pepper
  48 large round wonton or
    gyoza wrappers
2 tablespoons sesame oil (or as
  needed for frying)

Finely chop up the kimchi and chives. Wrap the tofu in a cheesecloth and firmly squeeze out the moisture.

Place the ground pork, kimchi, chives, tofu and ingredients from 🅐 in a bowl, and knead them together by hand. Then divide the mixture into 48 equal parts. Place a portion of filling in the middle of a wrapper. Wet the edge of the circle and fold it into a crescent, sealing the edges together. Next, bring the corners around to meet each other and use water to seal the ends together as well.

Heat 1 tablespoon of the sesame oil in a frying pan over medium heat. Add half of the pot stickers and ⅔ cup (150 ml) water to the pan. Cover and cook for 5 to 6 minutes. When most of the water has evaporated, remove the lid and fry for 2 to 3 more minutes, until the pot stickers are golden brown on the bottom. Repeat the procedure with the remaining sesame oil and pot stickers.

Cook the pot stickers in batches. If you plan to freeze them, freeze them on a tray, then transfer them to a freezer storage bag. The pot stickers will last up to a month in the freezer.

TIP

Form your pot stickers into a circular shape for an authentic Korean look!

Make a crescent moon shape, then fold the ends together to get a circular shape. This shape resembles a coin and is considered good luck in Korea.

Garlic Fried Chicken MANEUL

Piping hot fried chicken covered in garlic sauce, Korean style.

[Serves 4]

1½ lbs (700 g) boneless chicken thighs
Ⓐ 2 teaspoons soy sauce
  ½ teaspoon salt
  2 teaspoons sake or cooking sherry
  ⅛ teaspoon coarse freshly ground
    black pepper
6 tablespoons all-purpose flour
Cooking oil for deep frying
8–10 cloves garlic, outer skins intact
Ⓑ 3 tablespoons sesame oil
  ½ teaspoon salt
  ¼ teaspoon coarse freshly ground
    black pepper

Cut the chicken into chunks, place them in a bowl, and rub in the ingredients from Ⓐ. Dredge the seasoned chicken in the flour to coat evenly.

In a large, heavy-bottomed frying pan, heat 2 in (5 cm) of cooking oil to 340°F (170°C). Use tongs or chopsticks to place the chicken in the oil. Place the unpeeled garlic cloves in between the chicken pieces. Fry the garlic for 2 minutes and the chicken for 5 to 6 minutes until crisp, turning the pieces over occasionally to cook both sides, then transfer to a rack or plate with paper towels to drain.

Peel the garlic cloves and place them in a small bowl, then crush the garlic with a fork. Mix in the ingredients from Ⓑ.

Transfer the fried chicken to a serving plate and smear the garlic sauce evenly over them.

TIP

Peel the garlic cloves while hot

The thin skins on the garlic comes off easily when the garlic is hot. However, garlic right out of the pan is extremely hot, so be careful not to burn yourself.

Frying Pan

Total time
25 min

Seasoned Hamburgers in Gochujang Sauce

Gochujang red chili bean paste works surprisingly well with Worcestershire sauce and ketchup!

[Serves 4]

2 potatoes
1 carrot
½ head broccoli (about 7 oz/200 g)
1½ lbs (700 g) ground beef or pork
½ white onion, peeled and diced
2 eggs
A ½ cup (30 g) panko bread-
  crumbs
  1 teaspoon salt
  ¼ teaspoon freshly ground
  black pepper
1 tablespoon vegetable oil
B 2 tablespoons *gochujang* red
  chili bean paste
  2 tablespoons Worcestershire
  sauce
  2 tablespoons tomato ketchup
  2 teaspoons soy sauce

Cut the potato into bite-size chunks. Cut the carrot at alternating angles into small chunks of about the same size. Run them both under water and place on a microwave-safe plate. Cover and microwave on high for about 2 minutes, not letting the vegetables get too soft.

Separate the broccoli into florets. Bring 1 cup (250 ml) salted water to a boil in a saucepan and steam the broccoli quickly for 40 seconds, then drain.

Combine the ground meat, onion, eggs and ingredients from **A** in a bowl, and knead them together by hand. Split the mixture into eighths and shape them into patties.

Heat the oil in a frying pan over medium heat, then add the meat and cook for about 2 minutes. When one side has browned, turn over and cook for about another minute.

Add the ingredients from **B** and the prepared potato and carrot. Stir and cover the pan, lower the heat, and simmer for 2 to 3 minutes. Add the prepared broccoli, quickly stir to combine, and remove from the heat.

Microwave   Saucepan   Frying Pan   Total time 30 min

TIP

Gochujang is a secret weapon in your kitchen arsenal!

Gochujang isn't just spicy, it also has a sweetness and a depth of flavor all its own. Adding it to sauces provides richness and flavor.

Korean-style Gratin Chicken and Vegetables

If you add *gochujang* chili paste to white sauce, it tastes like a rich pizza sauce!

[Serves 4]

2 carrots, peeled
2 potatoes, peeled
1 small turnip, peeled
1 lb (450 g) boneless chicken
   thighs
1 tablespoon vegetable oil
Ⓐ 1 can (10½ oz/310 g) white
   sauce
   1 tablespoon *gochujang* red
   chili bean paste
¾ cup (85 g) shredded pizza
   cheese
Dried parsley, to garnish

Cut the vegetables into small, irregular chunks. Add them to a pot, cover with water, and place over medium-high heat. Bring to a boil and cook for about 2 minutes, then drain well.

Cut the chicken into bite-size pieces. Heat the oil in a frying pan over medium heat, then place the chicken in the pan, skin-side-down, and cook for 3 to 4 minutes. When it no longer sticks, turn over and cook for another 1 to 2 minutes on the other side. Add the prepared vegetables and stir-fry everything for 1 to 2 minutes more.

Mix the ingredients from Ⓐ together, then add them to the pan. Stir to combine, then pour everything into a 9 x 9 in (23 x 23 cm) casserole dish. Top with the cheese.

Broil on high for 5–6 minutes until the top becomes golden brown. Sprinkle the parsley on top as a final touch before serving.

TIP

Cheese and *gochujang* are a match made in heaven!

As both are cultured foods, cheese and *gochujang* are a perfect combination. The cheese softens the heat of the chili bean paste.

Pot
Frying Pan
Toaster Oven
Total time
30 min

TIP

Add the chili pepper and sesame seeds at the start of cooking

If you decorate the tofu and oysters with the sliced chili pepper and sesame seeds right when you begin cooking, they will be less likely to fall off.

Frying Pan | Total time 20 min
※ Not including marinating time

Assorted Jeon Seafood and Vegetable Fritters

Various ingredients covered in a light egg coating and pan-fried until crispy. You can add white fish fillets also!

[Serves 4]

12 large raw oysters, shucked
2 tablespoons salt
1 block firm tofu, about 10 oz (300 g)
2 king oyster mushrooms or shiitake mushrooms
1 small zucchini
All-purpose flour, as needed, to dredge the ingredients
2 eggs, beaten
4 tablespoons sesame oil, divided
½ teaspoon thinly sliced fresh chili pepper, or to taste
½ teaspoon roasted white sesame seeds (See Ingredient Note on page 86)
Spicy Dipping Sauce, to serve (see page 18)

Gently mix the oysters and salt in a bowl by hand, rinse to remove any grit, then dry on paper towels.

Wrap the tofu in a paper towel and let it sit for about 30 minutes to remove the moisture, then cut it into eight slices.

Cut the mushrooms in half lengthwise and slice crosswise. Cut the zucchini into ¼-in (6-mm) rounds.

Place some flour on a plate and lightly dredge the oysters, tofu and mushrooms then dip them in the beaten egg. Heat half of the sesame oil in a frying pan, add the mushrooms and zucchini, and fry over medium-low heat for 1-2 minutes on each side. Drain on a rack or a plate covered with paper towels. Add the remaining oil and repeat with the tofu and oysters, scattering the chili pepper and sesame seeds on top before turning them. Drain.

Transfer everything to a serving plate and serve with Spicy Dipping Sauce on the side.

TIP

Cook the oysters immediately after coating them

Oysters will dry out after being dipped in flour and egg. Heat the sesame oil in the pan first, then coat the oysters and lay them in the pan right away.

 If your pan won't hold all the ingredients as directed, use more sesame oil and fry the ingredients in three or four batches.

Stir-fried Vegetables and Squid with Bonito Flakes

This is a popular Korean dish. The umami of the squid and the bonito flakes make a mouthwatering combination!

[Serves 4]

1½ lbs (675g) whole fresh squid
1–2 slender Japanese eggplants (5–10 oz/150–300 g)
12 green beans
½ white onion
2 tablespoons sesame oil

Ⓐ 1½ teaspoons sugar
2 tablespoons soy sauce
1 tablespoon Korean red pepper powder or ground red pepper, or more to taste

½ cup (5 g) dried bonito flakes

Pull the tentacles of the squid from the bodies and remove the cartilage. Wash and dry them and cut into ¼-in (6-mm) rings. Cut off the entrails, eyes and beak attached to the tentacles, and then slice off the hard suction cups. Cut the tentacles into bite-size pieces.

Cut off the ends of the eggplants and halve them lengthwise. Cut in half crosswise, then slice lengthwise into spears. Cut off the tips of the green beans and slice them in half lengthwise. Cut the onion into thin wedges.

Heat the sesame oil in a frying pan over medium heat, add the vegetables, and stir-fry for about 2 minutes. Then add the squid and fry everything together.

When the squid turns slightly white, add the ingredients from Ⓐ and remove the pan from the heat. Sprinkle in the bonito flakes and lightly mix everything together. Serve hot with rice.

Frying Pan

Total time
25 min

P

Add the bonito flakes at the end after turning off the heat

Sprinkle in the bonito flakes at the end as a finishing touch. If you add them after removing the pan from the heat, the flavor will come through more clearly.

You can easily remove the tentacles from the body of the squid by inserting your thumb into the body. The beak is on the underside of where the tentacles attach.

Spicy Octopus Stir-fry

The chewy texture of the octopus and spicy-sweet *gochujang* sauce are irresistible!

[Serves 4]

½ white onion

½ carrot

10 oz (300 g) cooked octopus or scallops, sliced into bite-size chunks

🅐 4 tablespoons *gochujang* red chili bean paste

1 tablespoon Korean red pepper powder or ground red pepper, or more to taste

2 teaspoons soy sauce

2 teaspoons sugar

1 teaspoon minced garlic

8 oz (225 g) thin wheat-flour noodles (*somyeon*), dried

1 tablespoon sesame oil

Few sprigs of watercress or parsley, cut into short lengths

Store-bought cooked octopus is a convenient alternative when you're short on time. Look for it in the sushi section of Asian markets or at the seafood counter in larger grocery stores.

Slice the onion into thin wedges. Cut the carrot into thin sticks. Cut the octopus into bite-size chunks.

Combine the ingredients from 🅐 and mix well.

Cook the noodles according to the directions on the package, then rinse them in cool running water and drain well.

Heat the sesame oil in a frying pan over medium heat and stir-fry the carrot and onion for 1 to 2 minutes.

When the vegetables are just tender, add the octopus and the sauce mixture 🅐 and quickly stir-fry together. Finally, add the watercress or parsley and stir together gently from the bottom of the pan.

Arrange the stir-fry in the center of a serving plate and surround it with the cooked, drained noodles.

TIP

Somyeon noodles go really well with this dish

In Korea, it is common for this dish to be served with *somyeon* because the noodles are cool and bland and combine well with the fiery sauce. Mix the stir-fry with the noodles before eating to make the seasoning less intense.

Pot

Frying Pan

Total time
25 min

Cod Simmered in Gochujang Sauce

In Korea, *gochujang* is even used to flavor fish. It really enhances the flavor of cod!

[Serves 4]

1 bunch mustard greens or bok choy
1 cup (240 ml) water
½ cup (125 ml) sake or rice wine
4 fresh cod fillets
Ⓐ ½ teaspoon minced garlic
2 tablespoons *gochujang* red chili bean paste
2 tablespoons miso
1 teaspoon Korean red pepper powder or ground red pepper, or more to taste

Wash the greens and cut them into 2-in (5-cm) pieces.

Bring 1 cup of water and the sake to a boil in a large saucepan, then add the cod fillets.

When the liquid returns to a boil, stir in the ingredients from Ⓐ and simmer over medium-low heat for about 7–10 minutes. Then add the greens around the edges of the pot, cook for 2–3 more minutes until tender, and turn off the heat.

Serve with the greens on the side.

This recipe is also delicious with mackerel or beltfish!

TIP

Add the cod after the liquid begins boiling

If you add the cod after the liquid starts to boil, it won't smell fishy. The sake also helps to eliminate the fishy odor.

Saucepan

Total time
15 min

Fresh Tuna with Spicy Gochujang Dressing

Like a spicy Korean tuna tartare, this dish really brings out the taste of the tuna. It's delicious over white rice! (The raw egg yolk on top is optional.)

[Serves 4]

12 oz (350 g) sashimi-grade fresh tuna

½ apple

10 Korean perilla leaves or shiso leaves

Ⓐ 2 tablespoons *gochujang* red chili bean paste

1 tablespoon soy sauce

2 teaspoons sesame oil

2 teaspoons sugar

2 teaspoons rice vinegar or 1 teaspoon wine vinegar

¼ teaspoon roasted white sesame seeds (See Ingredient Note on page 86)

4 egg yolks (optional)

Cut the tuna into ¼-in (6-mm) strips. Cut the apple and perilla leaves into thin strips about the same width.

Combine the ingredients from Ⓐ in a large bowl and stir well. Add the tuna, apple slices and perilla strips and toss to mix.

Divide into 4 servings. Sprinkle each serving with sesame seeds and place one egg yolk in the middle, if using. Mix well before eating, just like a beef tartare.

TIP

Pull the knife toward you when slicing the tuna

Place the tuna on a cutting board with the thicker side furthest from you. As you slice the fish, keep the blade straight and pull the knife toward you to cut each piece.

✖ No cooking required

Total time 15 min

Fresh Squid Sashimi Salad HWE

Hwe means "raw fish" in Korean. Adding sesame oil and wasabi gives this dish a very Korean flavor.

[Serves 4]

10 oz (300 g) fresh squid, prepared for sashimi

2 green onions (scallions), white parts only

6 Korean perilla leaves or shiso leaves

Ⓐ 1 teaspoon sesame oil
½ teaspoon wasabi paste
¼ teaspoon salt

Use the body of the squid only and peel off the outer coating. Cut the squid into thin strips. Cut the green onions diagonally into thin slices and cut the perilla leaves into ½-in (1.25-cm) squares. Rinse with cold water, drain well and pat dry with a paper towel.

Combine the ingredients in Ⓐ and mix well to blend.

Place the squid and vegetables in a bowl and dress them with the mixture from Ⓐ. Toss well before serving.

Saucepan

Total time
25 min

Mackerel and Daikon Kimchi Stew

The kimchi, sake and ginger combine beautifully with the mackerel, and there is a huge amount of umami flavor packed into even a small serving of this stew!

[Serves 4]

½ daikon radish (about 10 oz/ 300 g)

2 cups (300 g) well-aged cabbage kimchi

A 4 cups (1 liter) Korean-style Fish Stock (see page 19) or 2 teaspoons dashi stock powder mixed with 4 cups (1 liter) water

6 tablespoons sake or cooking sherry

2 tablespoons soy sauce

1 tablespoon sugar

2 teaspoons peeled and grated fresh ginger

2 teaspoons minced garlic

2 teaspoons red pepper powder

¼ teaspoon salt

4 fresh mackerel fillets, or another oily fish (about 1½ lbs/675 g)

Peel the daikon and cut it into ½-in (1.25-cm) rounds. Cut the kimchi into bite-size pieces.

Lay the daikon on the bottom of a large saucepan and add the ingredients from **A**. Bring to a boil over medium heat. Add the mackerel and the kimchi, place a drop-lid on top, and let it simmer for about 15 minutes over medium-low heat.

Remove the drop lid and increase the heat to medium. Let it cook for a few more minutes until just a little liquid remains.

TIP

A drop lid allows more flavor to soak into the ingredients

When you use a Japanese drop lid, the lid covers the simmering broth, holding in the flavor so it permeates the entire dish. If you don't have access to a traditional wooden drop lid, you can improvise with a covering cut from parchment paper. Cut a hole in the middle to vent steam.

How to use well-aged and leftover kimchi

This is well-aged kimchi!

On the left side is kimchi that can be eaten plain; the kimchi on the right is well-aged. Notice how they look slightly different.

Well-aged kimchi

If you keep kimchi for a week or two in the fridge, it will continue to ferment and gradually become more sour. This sour kimchi is called "well-aged," and it goes well in boiled foods and stews like Hearty Pork and Potato Stew (page 38), Jjim (page 62) and Mackerel and Daikon Kimchi Stew (page 80). Try it in stir-fries like Sliced Pork Belly Stir-fried with Kimchi (page 67) as well. When you heat up sour kimchi, it loses its spiciness and acidity; the heat brings out a depth of flavor that makes a delicious final dish.

Leftover kimchi

Whether you eat it on noodles or with dressed meats and vegetables, there are lots of ways to finish up your kimchi. Below is a great way to enjoy kimchi in a ham and egg sandwich!

A recipe to use up your leftover kimchi

Kimchi Ham and Egg Sandwiches

This is a popular dish in Osaka's Korean district. The spiciness of kimchi goes perfectly with ham and eggs!

[Serves 4]

2 baby cucumbers
½ teaspoon salt
1 cup (160 g) cabbage kimchi
4 hard-boiled eggs
4 tablespoons mayonnaise
Butter, to spread on the bread
8 slices bread
4 slices ham

 The trick to keeping these sandwiches from getting soggy is to fully squeeze out the juice from the kimchi and the cucumber before you make the sandwiches.

Cut the cucumber in half lengthwise, then thinly slice them diagonally. Toss with the salt and let them stand for about 15 minutes, then firmly squeeze out the water. Chop the kimchi and squeeze out all the juice with your hand.

Peel and chop the hard-boiled eggs and mix with the mayonnaise.

Spread butter on one side of 4 slices of bread. Divide the egg, cucumber, kimchi and ham evenly and place it on each slice. Butter the remaining bread slices and place them on the fillings. Cut the sandwiches in half and serve.

Korean vegetable dishes are quick to prepare and very healthy!

Veggies prepared in a variety of ways!

Vegetable Side Dishes

When you go out to eat at a Korean restaurant, you'll be given many small vegetable dishes as starters. This custom of setting out lots of little sides like kimchi and other premade vegetable dishes is followed in the typical Korean household as well. This is why Korean cooking has many techniques to make vegetables delicious and to help you eat more of them. Try adding these recipes to your regular diet, and enjoy more vegetables currently in season!

Quick Water Kimchi

This refreshing dish is delicious down to the last drop. It's made with vinegar, so there's no fermenting required.

[Serves 2]

A 1 tablespoon salt
2 cups (500 ml) water
½ cup (125 ml) rice vinegar
½ carrot
1 small or ½ medium daikon radish (1 lb/450 g), peeled
1 rib celery
4 round slices lemon
3 cloves garlic, thinly sliced
Chili pepper threads, to garnish

Combine the ingredients from **A** in a saucepan and bring to a boil. Remove from heat and allow to cool to room temperature.

Meanwhile, quarter the carrot and daikon lengthwise, then slice them crosswise to make triangle-shaped slices. De-thread the celery and slice it thinly crosswise. Place the carrot, daikon and celery in a resealable food storage bag.

Remove the peel and seeds from the lemon slices and chop the flesh into small pieces. Add the lemon and sliced garlic to the bag.

When the **A** mixture is cool, pour it into the bag and seal. Refrigerate for about an hour to let the flavors mingle. When ready to serve, transfer the vegetables and liquid to a bowl and top with the chili pepper threads.

Saucepan

Total time	Storage
15 min	3~4 days

Water kimchi will keep for 3 to 4 days if refrigerated in a food-storage container.

Tip

What is water kimchi?

Traditional water kimchi is made by fermenting vegetables and other ingredients in water. The liquid is usually eaten along with the vegetables, and it is served like a cold soup. This is a very mild kimchi, as chili peppers are not used in its preparation. But traditional water kimchi includes even more beneficial probiotics than regular kimchi, so it is valued for its health benefits.

Fermentation can be complicated, however. The recipe given here is a quick version that lets you enjoy the refreshing taste of water kimchi made with vinegar and lemon.

Ingredient Note

Add some vibrant color to your dish!

Chili Pepper Threads

These dried red chili peppers, which are cut into fine threads, are only a little spicy. Their mild flavor and eye-catching color make them a go-to garnish in Korean cooking.

Tomato Kimchi

Fresh, juicy tomatoes are dressed in a sweet and spicy sauce for this quick recipe.

[Serves 4 as a side dish]

4 firm ripe tomatoes, about
    1 lb (450 g) total
4 to 5 thin green onion (scallion)
    shoots
2 tablespoons *gochujang* red chili
    bean paste
2 tablespoons rice vinegar

1 teaspoon soy sauce
1 teaspoon sugar
1 teaspoon sesame oil
1 teaspoon roasted white sesame
    seeds (see Ingredient Note)
½ teaspoon minced garlic
½ teaspoon peeled and grated
    fresh ginger

Slice each tomato into 8 wedges. Slice the green onions into ¾-in (2-cm) lengths.

Combine all the other ingredients in a bowl and mix well. Add the tomato and green onion and gently toss to coat with the dressing. These dried red chili peppers, which are cut into fine threads, are only a little spicy. Their mild flavor and eye-catching color make them a go-to garnish in Korean cooking.

Ingredient Note

To roast sesame seeds, add them to a heavy-bottomed saucepan and pour over just enough water to cover. Bring to a boil over medium heat. Lower the heat to a simmer and stir frequently until the water has nearly evaporated. Begin stirring continuously while occasionally tossing the seeds with a quick forward-and-back motion. Continue roasting until the seeds become fragrant and turn a pale golden color. Immediately transfer the seeds to a plate to avoid scorching them.

TIP

Choose firm tomatoes that won't get crushed

Fully ripe tomatoes are sweeter, but they also get squished more easily and tend to make the dish soggy. If you use slightly firm tomatoes, the final dish will look as good as it tastes.

X No cooking required

Total time 10 min

This kimchi loses moisture quickly, so it will not keep. Please enjoy it the same day you make it!

Quick Geotjeori Kimchi

Enjoy this fast, fresh kimchi as you would a lightly dressed salad.

[Serves 4]

¼ to ½ head napa cabbage (1 lb/450 g)

1 Japanese cucumber or baby cucumber

½ small carrot

4 round slices lemon

10 Korean perilla leaves or shiso leaves

1 tablespoon soy sauce

1 tablespoon Korean red pepper powder or ground red pepper

1 tablespoon sesame oil

2 tablespoons ground white sesame seeds

1 teaspoon minced garlic

¼ teaspoon salt

Separate and wash the napa cabbage leaves and cut them in diagonal slices to maximize the surface area by angling the knife across the center stems. Slice the cucumber thinly on the diagonal. Cut the carrot into fine matchsticks. Cut the lemon slices into quarters, and cut the perilla leaves into ½-in (1.25-cm) squares.

Combine all the other ingredients in a large bowl and mix well. Add the vegetables and stir gently to coat with the seasonings.

No cooking required

Total time
12 min

TIP

Mix the salad without crushing the vegetables

To preserve the crisp texture of the vegetables, mix them together thoroughly but gently. As when making Namul, it can be helpful to use your hands.

 Tip   **What is Geotjeori?**

In Korean, *geot* means "surface" and *jeori* means "pickled." This kimchi is prepared like a quick pickle and served like a salad, so it allows the freshness of the vegetables to really shine.

Potato and Kimchi Jeon Fritters

These simple, delicious potato pancakes make a great quick meal or snack.

[makes 8 small pancakes]

2 potatoes, about 8 oz (225 g) total

½ cup (60 g) all-purpose flour

¾ cup (125 g) napa cabbage kimchi

1 tablespoon sesame oil, divided

Peel the potatoes and grate them into a bowl. Add the flour and mix well.

Roughly chop the kimchi and add it to the potato.

Heat half the sesame oil in a large frying pan over medium heat. Pour half the batter to make 4 small pancakes and cook for 1 to 2 minutes. When the bottoms are lightly browned, turn the pancakes over and cook for another 1 to 2 minutes. Repeat with remaining oil and batter.

Frying Pan

Total time
15 min

TIP

Grated potato gives these pancakes a springy texture

The slightly chewy texture of these pancakes is from the grated potato. The Assorted Jeon Seafood and Vegetable Fritters on page 72 offer a very different texture for you to enjoy.

Frying Pan

Total time
10 min

Sweet & Salty Sardines with Green Bell Pepper

This mash-up of incredible flavors is a classic side dish found on dinner tables throughout Korea.

[Serves 4]

1 small green bell pepper
1 tablespoon sesame oil
½ cup (30 g) small dried sardines
Ⓐ ½ teaspoon minced garlic
2 teaspoons honey
2 teaspoons roasted white sesame seeds
   (See Ingredient Note on page 86)

Deseed and slice the bell pepper into thin strips.

Heat the sesame oil in a frying pan over low heat, then add the sardines and stir-fry. When they are crisp, add the bell pepper and stir-fry together.

Once the bell pepper is coated with oil, add the ingredients from Ⓐ one at a time. Continue stir-frying until most of the liquid has evaporated. Remove from heat. Sprinkle the roasted sesame seeds on top before serving.

Tip

You can substitute green shishito peppers for the bell peppers!

Sweet & Salty Sardines with Green Shishito Peppers
Ingredients and Directions

Remove and discard the stems of 4 green *shishito* peppers. Heat the sesame oil in a frying pan over medium heat, add the dried sardines and stir-fry. When crisp, add the peppers and stir-fry together. Add the ingredients from Ⓐ, but add 4 tablespoons of sake or rice wine and 2 teaspoons of *mirin* and use sugar instead of honey. Stir quickly to coat the peppers and sardines. Top with roasted sesame seeds.

Pot | Total time 25 min

Baby potatoes are very small new potatoes.

Braised Baby Potatoes

Get an energy boost from spicy potatoes and garlic scapes, piping hot!

[Serves 4]

20 baby potatoes (about 1 lb/450 g)
5–6 stalks garlic scapes or medium
   green onions (scallions)
Ⓐ ½ teaspoon minced garlic
   4 tablespoons soy sauce
   4 tablespoons sugar
   4 tablespoons sake or rice wine
   2 teaspoons Korean red pepper
      powder or ground red pepper
   2 teaspoons sesame oil
   2 cups (500 ml) water
1 teaspoon toasted white sesame seeds

Scrub the potatoes, leaving the skins on. Cut the garlic scapes or green onions into 1-in (2.5-cm) pieces.

Place the potatoes and the ingredients from Ⓐ in a pot over high heat. When the pot comes to a boil, reduce heat to medium and let the liquid reduce for about 15 minutes.

Stir in the garlic scapes and continue cooking until only a third of the liquid remains. Finally, sprinkle the sesame seeds and mix everything together before serving.

TIP

Vinegar keeps the flavor light

Adding vinegar cuts the rich taste of the soy sauce and *gochujang*, so the flavor isn't too strong.

Saucepan | Total time 30 min

Simmered Burdock Root or Turnip and Seaweed

This dish has a rich flavor imparted by soy sauce and *gochujang*, but it also has a refreshing aftertaste.

[Serves 4]

Two 4-in (10-cm) square sheets kombu seaweed

2 thin burdock roots or turnips (14 oz/400 g total)

Ⓐ 1½ cups (375 ml) water

2 tablespoons *gochujang* red chili bean paste

3 tablespoons soy sauce

3 tablespoons rice vinegar

3 tablespoons *mirin*

Cut the seaweed into ½-in (1.25-cm) squares. Peel the burdock roots or turnips and cut them into 1-in (2.5-cm) pieces, then soak them for about 5 minutes in a mixture of 2 tablespoons vinegar and 4 cups (1 liter) water (not included in ingredient list).

Spread the kombu pieces over the bottom of a medium saucepan. Drain and dry the burdock or turnip pieces and place them in the saucepan as well. Add the ingredients from Ⓐ and bring to a boil over medium heat. Cook for about 20 minutes, or until the liquid is reduced by two-thirds.

Korean Potato Salad

Add depth and richness to your usual potato salad with *gochujang*.

[Serves 4]

2 Japanese cucumbers or baby cucumbers

¼ onion

½ teaspoon salt

4 waxy white potatoes (about 1¼ lbs/600 g total)

Ⓐ 2 teaspoons rice vinegar
½ teaspoon salt
Pinch of freshly ground black pepper

4 slices ham

Ⓑ 6 tablespoons mayonnaise
1 tablespoon *gochujang* red chili bean paste

Red chili threads, to garnish (optional)

Cut the cucumber and onion into thin slices, toss in a bowl with the salt, and leave them for about 15 minutes. Then, lightly squeeze out and discard the moisture.

Wash the potatoes, leaving the skins on. Wrap in plastic wrap and microwave on high for about 3 minutes. Turn them over and microwave for 2 minutes more. While the potatoes are still hot, rub with a dry cloth to peel off the skin. Place the peeled potatoes in a bowl, crush them with a fork, and mix in the ingredients from Ⓐ. Allow to cool.

Slice the ham into small pieces. When the potatoes have cooled, add the vegetables, the ham and the mixed ingredients from Ⓑ. Transfer to a serving bowl and top with chili pepper threads if desired.

TIP

***Gochujang* pairs really well with mayonnaise**

Gochujang isn't just spicy. It also has a sweetness and umami flavor that complements mayonnaise well. Together, they are delicious!

Microwave | Total time 15 min

Spicy Gochujang Caprese Salad

The tangy, spicy dressing creates a new take on this classic Italian salad.

[Serves 4]

2 ripe tomatoes
7 oz (200 g) fresh mozzarella cheese
8 Korean perilla leaves or shiso leaves

A 2 tablespoons *gochujang* red chili bean paste
1 tablespoon soy sauce
2 teaspoons sesame oil
2 teaspoons sugar
2 teaspoons rice vinegar

Cut the tomato and cheese into ¼-in (6-mm) slices. Cut the perilla leaves into large squares.

Arrange the tomatoes, cheese and perilla on a serving dish in alternating sequence.

Combine the ingredients from **A** and stir well to blend. Drizzle the dressing over the salad.

No cooking required

Total time
5 min

TIP

Tangy *gochujang* dressing is perfect for a refreshing salad

The dressing used in this recipe is a variation on the classic Korean condiment *chogochujang* (see page 18). The acidity of this sauce goes nicely with salads, sashimi and vegetable dishes.

Muchim Grilled Beef Salad

This hearty salad is filled with satisfying meat and healthy fresh vegetables.

[Serves 4]

1 lb (450 g) beef, thinly sliced
2 tablespoons Super Tasty Sauce
    (page 18, or use store-bought
    yakiniku sauce)
10 lettuce leaves
4 green onions (scallions)

Ⓐ 1 tablespoon soy sauce
   2 teaspoons sesame oil
   1 teaspoon sugar
   1 teaspoon Korean red pepper
       powder or ground red pepper
1 teaspoon sesame oil
1 sheet *gim* seasoned nori, torn into
    pieces

Place the sliced beef in a bowl and rub the Super Tasty Sauce into it.

Tear the lettuce leaves. Cut the green onions into 1½-in (3.75-cm) lengths and slice them lengthwise into thin slivers. Combine the ingredients from Ⓐ in a separate bowl and mix well.

Heat the sesame oil in a frying pan over high heat, then fry the beef for 1 to 2 minutes, until cooked through.

Place the lettuce and green onion into a serving bowl and arrange the cooked beef on top. Drizzle the dressing from Ⓐ over, then scatter pieces of seaweed on top. Toss well before serving.

| Frying Pan | Total time 15 min |

 You can buy bottled *yakiniku* barbecue sauce or use the recipe on page 18 to make your own Super Tasty Sauce to marinate the meat.

TIP

Thoroughly toss the salad to fully enjoy the flavors

Muchim means to "mix" or "coat" in Korean. If you mix the salad well before eating it, the flavors of the meat, vegetables and dressing will mingle and taste even better.

Zippy Gochujang Pickled Vegetables

Slightly spicy and refreshing! Add *gochujang* for a uniquely Korean flavor. These pickles go really well with rice and beef or fish.

[Serves 4]

8 pearl onions
1 rib celery
1 red bell pepper
1 yellow bell pepper
1 clove garlic

 1 cup (250 ml) rice vinegar
1 cup (250 ml) water
4 teaspoons sugar
2 tablespoons *gochujang* red chili bean paste
1 teaspoon salt

Saucepan   Total time 18 min

Peel the pearl onions under lukewarm water, then cut them in half vertically. De-thread the celery and cut it into ½-in (1.25-cm) pieces. Remove the core and seeds from the bell peppers, then cut them into large triangular chunks by alternating the angle of the knife blade. Slice the garlic thinly crosswise. Transfer all the vegetables to a heat-resistant 1-quart (1-liter) jar.

In a small stainless steel or enameled saucepan, combine the ingredients from and place over medium heat. Bring to a boil, then remove from the heat. Allow the liquid to cool, then pour it over the vegetables. Let the pickles stand for about 1 hour before serving them so the flavors can develop.

These pickles will keep for about a week in the refrigerator.

TIP

Boil the pickling liquid to dissolve the sugar

Sugar is does not dissolve easily in vinegar, but if you stir it into the pickling liquid and bring it to a boil, it will dissolve. Let it cool before pouring it over the vegetables.

Assorted Namul Seasoned Vegetables

Use a variety of vegetables to create a rainbow of bright colors! This is also a perfect way to use up leftover vegetables.

[Serves 4]
Vegetable Ingredients
(make each separately)

½ small daikon radish (about 8 oz/225 g)
1 or 2 slender Japanese eggplants (about 7 oz/200 g)
7 oz (200 g) *shimeji* (beech) mushrooms
16–20 okra pods (about 10 oz/300 g)
24 cherry tomatoes (about 1 lb/450 g)
Salt, sesame oil, Korean red pepper powder or ground red pepper and roasted white sesame seeds (see page 86), as needed

Namul Seasoning
(make one portion for each vegetable; amount below is for only one)

Ⓐ 2 teaspoons sesame oil
1 teaspoon minced garlic
½ teaspoon salt
Pinch of sugar, to taste

Saucepan   Frying Pan   Total time 5~25 min

Daikon Namul
Use a mandoline or box grater to cut the daikon into fine shreds. Heat 1 teaspoon sesame oil in a frying pan over medium heat, then stir-fry the daikon for 1 or 2 minutes, until tender.

Strain well, then transfer to a bowl. Dress with the ingredients from Ⓐ and add a pinch of Korean red chili pepper powder or ground red pepper.

Egglant Namul
Slice the eggplant into small chunks, coat them with a pinch of salt and let them sit for about 10 minutes. Then squeeze out and discard the water and drain on paper towels.

Heat 1 teaspoon of sesame oil in a frying pan over medium heat. Stir-fry the eggplant for about 2 minutes, and then toss with the ingredients from Ⓐ to dress.

Shimeji Mushroom Namul
Cut off the hard ends of the mushrooms and split them apart into bite-size clusters.

Bring 2 cups (500 ml) of water and a pinch of salt to boil in a saucepan. Blanch the mushrooms for about 1 minute, then drain well. Transfer to a bowl and dress with the ingredients from Ⓐ.

Okra Namul
Remove the stem ends and slice each okra pod diagonally into 4 equal pieces.

Bring 2 cups (500 ml) of water and a pinch of salt to a boil in a saucepan. Blanch the okra until it turns bright green, then drain well. Transfer to a bowl and dress with the ingredients from Ⓐ.

Cherry Tomato Namul
Slice each cherry tomato in half.

Transfer the tomatoes to a bowl and dress with the ingredients from Ⓐ. Sprinkle sesame seeds on top.

TIP

Let the mushrooms get slightly dry

When you partially dry mushrooms, the flavor becomes more concentrated as they lose moisture. On a clear day, set the mushrooms out in the sun for 2 to 6 hours, until the outside of the mushrooms becomes dry, but not so much that they dry out completely.

Frying Pan

Total time
20 min

※ Does not include drying time

Seasoned Mushrooms

Partially dry a variety of different mushrooms to intensify their umami flavor! This method of preparing mushrooms also gives them a delightful texture.

[Serves 4]

1¼ lbs (600 g) fresh assorted Japanese or Asian mushrooms like *enoki*, shiitake, *shimeji* and *maitake* (try to purchase equal amounts of 2 or 3 different kinds)

1 tablespoon sesame oil

Ⓐ 2 teaspoons finely minced garlic
1 teaspoon salt
4 tablespoons ground white sesame seeds

Cut away and discard the hard ends of the thin-stalk mushrooms like *enokitake* or *shimeji*, then separate the individual stalks in the clusters. For larger mushrooms like shiitake, cut off the hard ends of the stems and cut the caps and stems into bite-size slices.

Spread all the mushrooms out on a clean tray or basket and set in the sun to dry for 2 to 4 hours until partially dried.

Heat the sesame oil in a frying pan over medium heat. Add the mushrooms and stir-fry for 2 to 3 minutes, and then mix in the ingredients from Ⓐ.

Namul Salad Variations

From familiar vegetables high in beta carotene to root and even dried vegetables, any kind of vegetables can be made into *namul* to add one more course to your meal when friends drop by!

Quick Eggplant Salad

Whet your appetite with this dish that is loaded with green onion, garlic, sesame and red pepper!

[Serves 4]

2 slender Japanese eggplants (about 1 lb/450 g)
Ⓐ 2 tablespoons finely chopped green onion, white
    parts only
1 tablespoon soy sauce
1 teaspoon honey
1 teaspoon Korean red pepper powder or ground
    red pepper
1 teaspoon roasted white sesame seeds (see page 86)
1 teaspoon minced garlic
½ teaspoon salt

Cut off the stem ends of each eggplant, and wrap each one individually in plastic wrap. Microwave on high for about 2 minutes. Turn over and cook about 1 minute more. Plunge into cold water to cool.

Combine the ingredients from Ⓐ in a bowl and mix well to blend. Remove the plastic wrap from the eggplants and slice them lengthwise into long thin strips. Place them on a serving plate and drizzle the dressing over them.

Microwave | Total time 10 min

Cucumber Salad with Sesame Dressing

The deep richness of tahini sesame paste makes a delicious accompaniment to crunchy cucumbers.

[Serves 4]

4 Japanese cucumbers
½ teaspoon salt
Ⓐ ½ teaspoon finely minced garlic
2 tablespoons tahini or ground sesame
    seeds
1 teaspoon soy sauce
Pinch of salt
1 teaspoon sesame oil

Cut the cucumbers into very thin slices and sprinkle with the salt. Leave for about 10 minutes until soft. Squeeze gently to remove the moisture, place in a bowl, and dress with the ingredients from Ⓐ.

No cooking required | Total time 15 min

Warm Seasoned Zucchini

Zucchini is very popular in Korea.

[Serves 4]

2 slender zucchini, about 10 oz (300 g)
2 teaspoons sesame oil
Ⓐ 1 teaspoon finely minced garlic
1 teaspoon Korean red pepper powder or ground red pepper
½ teaspoon salt
1 tablespoon ground black sesame seeds

Cut the zucchini in half lengthwise and slice into ¼-in (5-mm) half moons.

Heat the sesame oil in a frying pan over medium heat. Add the zucchini and stir-fry until just soft, then add the ingredients from Ⓐ one at a time, stirring gently after each addition.

Frying Pan

Total time
12 min

Seasoned Tomato Salad

Fresh tomatoes are simply wonderful in *namul*!

[Serves 4]

¼ white onion
2 or 3 ripe tomatoes, about 1 lb (450 g)
Ⓐ ½ teaspoon finely minced garlic
½ teaspoon salt
1 teaspoon sesame oil
1 teaspoon ground white sesame seeds

Cut the onion into thin slices. Soak in cold water, then drain and dry.

Cut each tomato into 6 wedges, then into triangular chunks. Mix the ingredients from Ⓐ and add to the tomato. Transfer to a serving bowl and top with the sliced onions.

No cooking required

Total time
10 min

Grilled Vegetable Salad

The trick to making these vegetables delicious is to bring out their sweetness through grilling!

Small Grill | Total time 8 min

[Serves 4]

1 lotus root or turnip, peeled
1 carrot, peeled
1 slender Japanese eggplant
2 large king oyster or shiitake mushrooms
Ⓐ 1 teaspoon finely minced garlic
  1 teaspoon soy sauce
  ¼ teaspoon salt
  1 tablespoon sesame oil
2 teaspoons ground white sesame seeds

Peel the lotus root or turnip and slice thinly. Soak in 2 cups (500 ml) water mixed with 1 tablespoon rice vinegar (not included in ingredient list) for 5 minutes. Cut the carrot diagonally into thin slices. Cut the eggplant diagonally into thin slices and soak in water for about 5 minutes. Thinly slice the mushrooms.

Drain and dry the soaked vegetables. Cover the grill with foil and arrange the vegetables on it. Grill on both sides, taking care not to burn them. Mix together the ingredients in Ⓐ to make the dressing.

Pour the dressing over the vegetables while they are still hot. Toss well, then transfer to a serving plate and sprinkle with sesame seeds.

Korean Green Salad

The *namul* seasonings make for a uniquely delicious salad.

[Serves 4]

Package of fresh baby salad greens, about 8 oz (225 g)
Ⓐ ½ teaspoon of finely minced garlic
  1 teaspoon Korean red pepper powder or ground red pepper
  1 teaspoon soy sauce
  1 teaspoon sesame oil
  1 teaspoon ground white sesame seeds
  ¼ teaspoon salt

Remove any hard stems from the greens, wash and dry in a spinner.

Mix the ingredients from Ⓐ in a bowl to make the dressing. Dress the greens just before eating.

No cooking required | Total time 5 min

Frying Pan

Total time
5 min

※ Not including soaking time

Dried Daikon Salad

The pleasantly crunchy texture of *kiriboshi* (dried daikon radish) makes this a wonderful dish, so it is worth the trouble of ordering it.

[Serves 4]

3½ oz (100 g) packet of *kiriboshi* dried daikon radish strips
2 teaspoons sesame oil
Ⓐ ½ teaspoon finely minced garlic
⅓ teaspoon salt
½ teaspoon chicken stock powder
2 tablespoons ground black sesame seeds

Briefly rinse the dried daikon, then set it in a bowl and cover with water. Let it soak for about 20 minutes to rehydrate, then remove from the bowl and lightly squeeze out the extra water.

Heat the sesame oil in a frying pan over medium heat. Add the daikon and stir-fry for 1 to 2 minutes. Add the ingredients from **Ⓐ** to season. Mix in the sesame seeds and transfer to a serving bowl.

Tip

Mix the namul *vegetables and seasonings by hand!*

Tossing the vegetables and seasonings together by hand makes the best-tasting *namul*. To fully blend the flavors and evenly coat the vegetables, I highly recommend mixing with both hands instead of using utensils like spoons or chopsticks. Each person has a different style of doing this in Korea and the Korean language has a term to describe this: "the taste of your hands." When mixed by hand, your homemade *namul* will be especially delicious!

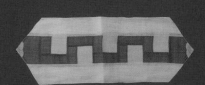

Chapter 4

Korean hot pots, soups and stews are delicious and give you stamina!

Dishes filled with both flavor and nutrition— your body will thank you!

Hot Pots and Soups

Soups are essential in Korean home cooking. The various ingredients' flavors mingle together and permeate the body, healing our fatigue. Here are some easy recipes for hot pot dinners that pack a punch, and some soups for those days that you need a tasty side dish.

TIP

Use a paper towel to pick up extra grease

Stir-frying releases the pork's flavor, but it also renders out excess fat. Use a folded paper towel held between cooking chopsticks to blot it up.

TIP

Stir-fry the kimchi to concentrate its flavor

I use well-aged kimchi for a stronger kimchi flavor. Lightly stir-frying the kimchi before simmering removes the sourness, leaving a hearty kimchi taste.

Pot | Total time 30 min

Hearty Kimchi Jjigae Stew

This Korean staple is filled with the robust flavors of braised pork and kimchi.

[Serves 4]

1¼ cups (200 g) well-aged cabbage kimchi
10 oz (300 g) pork belly, thinly sliced
6–8 green onions (scallions), trimmed
1 block firm tofu, about 14 oz (400 g)
1 tablespoon sesame oil
One 1-in (2.5-cm) piece fresh ginger, peeled and thinly sliced
2 cloves garlic, peeled and thinly sliced
6 cups (1.5 liters) Korean-style Fish Stock (see page 19) or other stock
A 3 tablespoons *gochujang* red chili bean paste
1 tablespoon soy sauce
Fresh chili peppers (red or green), thinly sliced diagonally, as desired to garnish (optional)

Cut the kimchi and pork into small pieces. Cut the white parts of the green onions diagonally into ½-in (1.25-cm) pieces.

Cut the tofu in half lengthwise and then crosswise into ½-in (1.25 cm) slices.

Heat the sesame oil in a large pot over medium heat. Add the pork and cook until the fat is rendered out. Drain off the excess grease.

Add the kimchi, green onion, ginger and garlic, and lightly stir-fry.

Add the stock and bring to a boil. Skim off the foam, then stir in the ingredients from **A**. Add the tofu and cook for another 5 minutes. Remove from heat and garnish with sliced chili peppers before serving.

Korean-style Fish Stock (see page 19) provides the most authentic taste! An instant powdered version is available from online suppliers. Other soup stocks like vegetable stock and Japanese dashi stock also work well. You can buy instant dashi stock powder online.

Fish and Daikon Hot Pot

Daikon radish is delicious when it absorbs the rich flavor of fresh fish!

[Serves 4]

2 lbs (1 kg) fish scraps (salmon, cod, etc.) left over after filleting
1 small daikon radish or ½ medium daikon (about 1¼ lbs/ 600 g), peeled
6–8 green onions (scallions), trimmed
Small bunch watercress, chives or parsley
1 clove garlic

Ⓐ 2 quarts (2 liters) Korean-style Fish Stock (see page 19), or dashi stock made from instant dashi stock powder
2 tablespoons *gochujang* red chili bean paste
2 tablespoons Korean red pepper powder or ground red pepper
2 teaspoons salt

 Crush the garlic with the thickest part of the blade, away from the cutting edge!

Briefly blanch the fish scraps, then rinse in cold water. Drain well.

Cut the daikon into ½ in (1.25 cm) thick bars. Quarter each green onion lengthwise and then cut into 1½-in (3.75-cm) pieces. Slice the watercress or chives or parsley into pieces. Crush the garlic with the flat side of the knife.

Combine the ingredients from **Ⓐ** in a large pot over medium heat. Add the daikon radish and garlic, bring to a boil, then let simmer for 5 minutes.

Add the drained fish scraps and the green onion. Cook for another 5 minutes. Add the watercress or chives or parsley and simmer briefly. Remove from the heat and serve hot.

Pot | Total time 30 min

TIP

Briefly blanch and rinse the fish before adding them to the hot pot

Blanch the fish until it changes color, then rinse it gently in cold water to get rid of impurities, fat and blood. This will greatly improve the flavor of the stock.

Samgyetang Chicken Soup with Rice

This soup is restorative and energizing. Chicken wings are so easy to cook, too!

[Serves 4]

6 chicken wings

6 tablespoons uncooked glutinous rice

1 dried ginseng root

4 green onions (scallions), white parts only

1 small turnip, carrot or potato, peeled

2 cloves garlic

12 boiled ginkgo nuts

Ⓐ 4 cups (1 liter) water
1½ teaspoons salt
¼ teaspoon freshly ground black pepper

4 tablespoons pine nuts

Rinse the chicken wings. Wash the glutinous rice and leave it in a sieve for 15 minutes.

Quarter the ginseng root and cut in half lengthwise. Cut the green onions into 1-in (2.5-cm) lengths. Cut the turnip or carrot or potato into 1-in (2.5-cm) chunks and place them in water. Cut the garlic cloves in half and shell the ginkgo nuts.

Combine the ingredients from Ⓐ, and all the other ingredients except the pine nuts in a pot over medium heat. When it starts boiling, skim the foam off the top. Lower the heat and simmer for 20 minutes.

Dry roast the pine nuts in a frying pan over low heat until fragrant then remove from the heat and set aside. Add them just before serving the soup.

Pot

Total time 45 min

TIP

Use glutinous rice for a smooth taste and texture

Using glutinous rice will make the soup naturally thick and sweet. However, you can also use regular rice if you don't have glutinous rice available.

Pot | Total time 12 min

Clam and Chive Soup

A clear soup full of the savory taste of clams accented by the crunchy texture of chives.

[Serves 4]

10 oz (300 g) fresh baby clams in shell, or 1 small can clam meats
Ⓐ 4 cups (1 liter) water
4 tablespoons sake or rice wine
1 teaspoon minced garlic
¼ teaspoon pepper
Small handful of chives, about 1 oz (30 g)

Clean the clams as described on page 29. Wash under cold running water, rubbing the shells together, then drain and dry.

Combine the ingredients from Ⓐ in a pot over medium heat. Bring to a boil and add the clams, skimming off the foam.

Chop the chives into small pieces. Once the clams open, sprinkle the chives into the pot and turn off the heat.

Clams are rich in taurine, so they're great for when you're tired or hung over.

TIP

Skim off as much of the foam from the clams as possible

The secret to making this dish delicious is to carefully skim off the frothy white foam that comes from the clams. This will make the soup taste better.

Saucepan

Total time 8 min

In Korea, *wakame* seaweed soup is eaten by women right after they give birth, to fortify them. It's also eaten by children on their birthdays to show gratitude to their mother for giving birth to them.

Wakame Seaweed Soup

Wakame is rich in vitamins and minerals.

4 cups (1 liter) Korean-style Fish Stock (see page 19) or dashi stock made from instant dashi stock powder

Ⓐ 1 teaspoon minced garlic
½ teaspoon salt, or to taste

2 tablespoons dried *wakame* seaweed

2 green onions (scallions), white parts only, roughly chopped

2 teaspoons roasted white sesame seeds, to garnish (see page 86)

Bring the stock to a boil over medium heat, then add the ingredients from Ⓐ and the *wakame* seaweed.

When the *wakame* unfurls, turn off the heat. Sprinkle in the green onions and sesame seeds, and serve immediately.

TIP

You can add dried *wakame* seaweed directly into the saucepan!

It is absolutely fine to add dried *wakame* seaweed directly to the soup. This saves the trouble of washing and drying the *wakame* seaweed. When you don't have much time, you can also use instant stock powder like vegetable stock powder or dashi stock powder.

Saucepan | Total time 10 min

TIP

Gochujang goes well with miso!

Gochujang and miso are both fermented foods. When paired together, they create a wonderfully rich soup.

Spicy Gochujang Miso Soup with Mushrooms

Warm up your body with a bit of spice!

[Serves 4]

- 4 oz (100 g) *shimeji, enoki* or shiitake mushrooms
- 6 thin green onions (scallions)
- 4 cups (1 liter) Korean-style Fish Stock (see page 19) or dashi stock made with instant dashi stock powder
- **A** 2 tablespoons *gochujang* red chili bean paste
  3 tablespoons miso

Cut off the hard parts of the mushroom stems. If using *shimeji* or *enoki* mushrooms, separate the individual stalks. If using shiitake mushrooms, slice them thinly. Finely chop the green onions.

Bring the stock to a boil in a saucepan over medium heat. Add the mushrooms. Once it returns to a boil, slowly mix in the ingredients from **A**.

Ladle the soup into individual serving bowls and sprinkle the green onion on top to serve.

 Adding the mushrooms early in the cooking process releases their flavor into the soup.

Tip **Mixing *gochujang* with other fermented products**

Gochujang, a traditional Korean seasoning, is made by mixing together glutinous rice, red pepper powder, soybeans and salt, and fermenting them. Pairing it with other fermented products such as miso, soy sauce and cheese creates deliciously complex flavors.

Bean Sprout Soup

This soup is eaten in Korea when you have a hangover. The bean sprouts are very chewy!

[Serves 4]

14 oz (400 g) fresh bean sprouts
5 cups (1.25 liters) Korean-style Fish
    Stock (see page 19) or dashi
    stock made with instant dashi
    stock powder
Ⓐ 1 teaspoon minced garlic
   1 teaspoon salt
Thinly sliced fresh red chili pepper,
    to garnish

Remove the tails and husks from the bean sprouts.

Bring the stock to a boil in a pot over medium heat. Add the bean sprouts and cook until tender. Stir in the ingredients from Ⓐ, reduce the heat to low and simmer for about 2 minutes.

Ladle into individual serving bowls and garnish with red pepper slices.

If cooked for too long, bean sprouts will lose their crunch, so simmer them briefly!

TIP

Remove the roots of the bean sprouts for a better taste

Taking extra time to remove the roots will make the bean sprouts more delicious and less watery, boosting their flavor to a whole new level.

Pot   Total time 10 min

Chilled Cucumber and Seaweed Soup

Perfect for a hot summer day! This soup is also an ideal foil for greasy foods.

[Serves 4]

1 Japanese cucumber or baby cucumber

¼ teaspoon salt

Ⓐ 4 cups (1 liter) water
  ½ teaspoon salt, or to taste
  2 teaspoons chicken or vegetable stock powder

4 tablespoons dried *wakame* seaweed

1 tablespoon rice vinegar

½ teaspoon roasted white sesame seeds, to garnish (see page 86)

Cut the cucumber in half lengthwise, then into very thin diagonal slices. Sprinkle the ¼ teaspoon salt over and massage it into the cucumber.

Heat the ingredients from Ⓐ in a saucepan over medium heat. Bring to a boil then add the *wakame*. When the seaweed unfurls, remove the soup from the heat and allow it to cool. Transfer to a storage container and refrigerate for 1 hour to chill.

To serve, squeeze out and discard the water from the salted cucumber. Add the cucumber and the vinegar to the soup. Serve in a bowl and sprinkle roasted sesame seeds on top.

 Taste the soup and adjust the amount of vinegar to suit your preference!

Saucepan | Total time 15 min

TIP

Remove the moisture from the cucumber by massaging it with salt and allowing it to sit

Massaging the cucumber slices with salt softens them and releases the water in the cucumber. This will make them more crunchy and the soup will have a better flavor.

Wakame and Dried Shrimp Soup

Tiny dried shrimp add flavor and color to this soup.

[Serves 4]

6 cups (1.5 liters) water
2 tablespoons tiny dried shrimp
4 tablespoons dried *wakame*
   seaweed
½ teaspoon salt, or to taste
1 large clove garlic, finely minced

If you can find Japanese *sakura* shrimp, you can add them directly to the soup. Other types of dried shrimp may need to be lightly ground before adding them (see note). Put 3 cups of water and the dried shrimp into a saucepan and place it over medium heat.

Once it boils, add the *wakame* seaweed, salt and garlic, and briefly let simmer. Remove from the heat and serve.

Japanese *sakura* dried shrimp are very light and tiny and can be added directly to the soup. Other types of dried shrimp are larger and heavier and need to be lightly ground in a mortar or food processor before adding them.

TIP

Add the dried shrimp to the saucepan before putting it on the heat, then add the *wakame* at the end

Adding the *sakura* shrimp to the pot first and then heating it up, brings out more of the umami in the shrimp. The *wakame* is added later and simmered only briefly.

Saucepan

Total time
10 min

TIP

Dissolve the miso in some cooked soup before adding it to the saucepan

I recommend dissolving the miso in a bit of the soup before adding it to the saucepan. This will allow the miso to spread throughout with the soup more quickly.

Saucepan

Total time
20 min

Korean-style Pork and Mushroom Miso Soup

I've modified this Korean miso hot pot to make a variation on the Japanese pork miso soup called *tonjiru*. The *gochujang* elevates this from good to phenomenal!

[Serves 4]

2 teaspoons sesame oil

2 tablespoons *gochujang* red chili bean paste

7 oz (200 g) pork, thinly sliced

2 large napa cabbage leaves

4 oz (100 g) fresh *maitake* or shiitake mushrooms

8 green onions (scallions), green parts only

6 cups (1.5 liters) Korean-style Fish Stock (see page 19) or dashi stock made with instant dashi stock powder

4 tablespoons miso

Rub the sesame oil and *gochujang* into the sliced pork to season it.

Cut the napa cabbage into 2-in (5-cm) squares. Tear or slice the mushrooms into bite-size pieces. Cut the green onions into ½-in (1.25-cm) lengths.

Bring the stock to a boil in a saucepan over medium heat.

Add in the pork, napa cabbage and mushrooms. Simmer for 4 to 5 minutes. Stir a bit of the soup into the miso to dissolve it, then add it into the saucepan. Add the green onion and simmer for another minute before removing from heat.

TIP

Add the rice cake after the soup starts boiling

One characteristic of Korean *tteok* is that it heats up quickly. It's best to add it after the soup is already boiling.

Pot

Total time
12 min

Korean Egg-drop Soup

Flat Korean rice cake is the star of the show but if you cannot find it, use firm tofu instead.

[Serves 4]

6 oz (175 g) *tteok* rice cakes or ½ block firm tofu (6 oz/175 g)
4 green onions, finely sliced
6 cups (1.5 liters) water
4 teaspoons beef or vegetable stock powder
½ teaspoon finely minced garlic
Ⓐ 2 teaspoons soy sauce
1 teaspoon salt, or to taste
2 eggs
½ sheet *gim* seasoned nori, to garnish
1 teaspoon ground white sesame seeds, to garnish

Briefly rinse the *tteok* rice cakes in water and drain well. If using firm tofu, slice it into cubes. Slice the green onions finely.

Combine the water and the stock powder in a pot and bring to a boil over medium heat. Add the *tteok* or tofu and garlic. Simmer for 2 to 3 minutes until the rice cakes soften. Add the ingredients from Ⓐ.

Whisk the eggs enough to break the yolks, then stir them into the pot. Turn off the heat.

Serve the soup in individual soup bowls. Garnish with the green onions, torn bits of seasoned nori and ground sesame seeds.

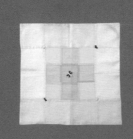

Chapter 5

These one-dish meals are hearty enough to leave you satisfied.

A whole meal packed into a single dish

Rice and Noodle Dishes

This is a collection of one-dish meals using rice or noodles that are hugely popular in Korea. They include meat, fish and vegetables, and are very nutritious and filling, so they're perfect for a leisurely lunch on your day off or for those evenings when you don't feel like making a variety of dishes for dinner. Whether you want a hit of spice or a milder taste, there are many flavors to choose from to suit your mood.

Kimchi Fried Rice

The spiciness and aroma are addictive! Mix the fried egg into the rice and enjoy.

[Serves 4]

1½ cups (250 g) cabbage kimchi
3 thin green onions (scallions)
1 tablespoon sesame oil
8 oz (225 g) ground beef or pork
4 cups (800 g) cooked rice
½ teaspoon salt, or to taste
½ teaspoon freshly ground black
    pepper, or to taste
4 eggs
Vegetable oil, for frying the eggs

Cut the kimchi into chunks. Finely chop the green onions.

Heat the sesame oil in a frying pan over medium heat. Add the meat and stir-fry until it browns. Add the kimchi and stir-fry to combine.

Add the rice and season with the salt and pepper. Continue to cook, stirring, until all ingredients are thoroughly mixed in.

Quickly stir in the green onion and turn off the heat. Divide evenly among four individual serving bowls.

Heat the vegetable oil in the frying pan over medium heat. Break in the eggs and fry them sunny side up. Top each serving of fried rice with an egg.

Ground pork, thinly sliced pork or ground beef are all great options for this dish!

Frying
Pan

Total time
15 min

Total time
10 min

This is a great way to serve sashimi with rice and vegetables all together in one dish!

Sashimi Rice Salad with Tomato and Gochujang Dressing

A refreshing way to serve sashimi, rice and fresh vegetables with a tangy spicy-sweet sauce.

[Serves 4]

6 oz (175 g) sashimi-grade fresh salmon or red snapper
Handful of alfalfa sprouts
16 cherry tomatoes
4 red-leaf lettuce leaves
4 cups (800 g) cooked rice
4 teaspoons sesame oil
Ⓐ 1 tablespoon *gochujang* red chili bean paste
1 tablespoon soy sauce
2 teaspoons sesame oil
2 teaspoons sugar
2 teaspoons rice vinegar
Mayonnaise, to taste (optional)

Thinly slice the fish at a 45-degree angle. Remove the roots of the sprouts. Discard the stem ends of the cherry tomatoes and slice the tomatoes in half. Tear apart the lettuce.

Spread one cup of the rice on a plate and drizzle 1 teaspoon of the sesame oil over it. Arrange one quarter of the fish, sprouts, tomatoes and lettuce on top, taking care to balance the colors. Mix the ingredients from Ⓐ together and drizzle one quarter of it over the salad. Top with a small amount of mayonnaise, if using. Make the other servings the same way.

TIP

Mixing the salad thoroughly before eating heightens the flavors

Much like the classic Korean Bibimbap, mixing this rice salad thoroughly allows the flavors to mingle, creating a superbly delicious dish.

Bulgogi Beef Barbecue Sushi Rolls

This Korean version of sushi rolls is perfect for box lunches or parties! Using plastic wrap instead of a sushi mat to roll the sushi is easier!

[Serves 4]

6 oz (175 g) beef, very thinly sliced

2 tablespoons *yakiniku* sauce or Super Tasty Sauce (see page 18)

1 teaspoon sesame oil

4 sticks (around 3 oz/80 g) mild cheese

1 cup (160 g) cabbage kimchi

4 red-leaf lettuce leaves

2 cups (400 g) cooked short grain rice

2 sheets (7½ x 8½ in/19 x 21 cm) toasted sushi nori

8 Korean perilla or shiso leaves, halved lengthwise

2 tablespoons mayonnaise

Sesame oil, as needed

Put the beef in a bowl and massage with the *yakiniku* sauce or Super Tasty Sauce. Heat the sesame oil in a frying pan over medium heat. Fry the meat for 1 to 2 minutes until cooked through, then remove from the heat.

Cut the cheese into bars. Cut the kimchi into bite-size pieces and squeeze to remove liquid. Tear the lettuce into large pieces.

Lay out a sheet of clear plastic wrap larger than the size of the nori sheets. Place a nori sheet on top of it. Spread half the rice over the nori, leaving 1 in (2.5 cm) clear across the top. Lay half of the lettuce in a row just below the center of the rice. Do the same with half of the beef, cheese, kimchi, perilla leaves and mayo. Roll the edge of the nori closest to you up tightly around the filling. Once you reach the far edge of the nori, pull back the plastic wrap from the bottom of the nori close to you. Repeat to make a second roll.

Brush a little sesame oil over the surface of the sushi using a brush or paper towel. Cut the rolls into bite-size pieces with a very sharp knife to serve.

Wipe the knife with a wet towel between cuts to make clean, even slices.

TIP

Peel back a bit of the plastic wrap so the uncovered nori at the far edge can stick to the nori edge nearest you

Lift up the edge of the plastic wrap closest to you and fold the nori and rice on the far side over the fillings then seal the nori together with a wet finger. Continue to roll the sushi tightly, peeling the plastic wrap off of the nori as needed so the two nori surfaces can seal it together tightly. Once you finish rolling the sushi, wrap the plastic wrap around it. Press on all sides and wait a bit for the flavors to mingle before slicing.

Frying Pan

Total time 15 min

Bite-size Sushi Salad Rolls

For these mini sushi rolls, all you have to do is slice the fillings and roll them up.

[Serves 4]

1½ oz (40 g) pickled daikon radish
1 Japanese cucumber or baby cucumber
2 teaspoons white sesame seeds
Sixteen 2 x 3-in (5 x 7.5-cm) sheets *gim* seasoned nori
1½ cups (300 g) cooked short grain rice
2 imitation crab meat sticks
Radish kimchi, to serve (optional)

Slice the pickled radish and cucumber into thin 2-in (5-cm) matchsticks.

Place sheets of seasoned nori vertically on a work surface. Spread a thin layer of rice over the lower ¾ of the nori, leaving the top ends empty as shown in the picture below. Sprinkle the sesame seeds over. Separate the crab sticks into thin strips and place the crab sticks, pickled radish and cucumber across the rice, just below the center. Wrap the nori and rice around the filling, starting from the end closest to you, sealing the roll with the uncovered nori.

Serve with radish kimchi on the side, if you like.

Pickled daikon radish is slightly sweet and crunchy and can be purchased in supermarkets that sell sushi. If you cannot find it, use any other sweet pickles and slice them into thin strips. You can also use thin strips of carrot or avocado in these rolls.

TIP

Only cover three-quarters of the nori with rice

Leave the top quarter of the nori free of rice. This makes it easier to roll it up.

Total time
10 min

No cooking required

Shrimp Rice Porridge

The texture of the shrimp with the flavors of ginger and sesame are irresistible!

[Serves 4]

1 cup (180 g) uncooked short grain rice
8 oz (225 g) peeled raw shrimp
½ zucchini
1 teaspoon sesame oil
1 teaspoon peeled and finely chopped fresh ginger
6 cups (1.5 liters) water
1 teaspoon chicken or vegetable stock powder
1 teaspoon salt, or to taste
4 eggs
Ground sesame seeds and *gim* seasoned nori, to taste

Wash and drain the rice. Let stand in a fine sieve for about 15 minutes.

Devein the shrimp. Cut the zucchini in quarters lengthwise, then slice into thin wedges.

Heat the sesame oil in a pot over medium heat. Add the shrimp and the ginger and stir-fry. Once the shrimp turn pink, add the water and chicken stock powder and simmer for 1 to 2 minutes. Remove and reserve the shrimp.

Add the rice to the pot. Let it simmer over low heat for 15 minutes, stirring periodically. Add the zucchini and the shrimp. Season with salt, to taste. Simmer for 1 minute, then turn off the heat.

Distribute the porridge among four bowls. Place an egg on top of each serving while the porridge is still very hot, so it can partially cook, then sprinkle ground sesame seeds and torn pieces of seasoned nori over as desired.

Rice porridge is a standard Korean food often eaten for breakfast.

Break the egg yolk and stir it into the dish as you eat it! If you prefer the egg slightly cooked, add it to the porridge while it is still cooking.

Pot

Total time
30 min

Black Sesame Rice Porridge

A rice porridge that is good for health and beauty, used in Korean medicinal cooking.

[Serves 4]

1 cup (180 g) uncooked short grain rice
6 cups (1.5 liters) water
6 tablespoons black sesame paste
1 tablespoon pine nuts
Salt and sugar, to taste

Wash and drain the rice. Let stand in a fine sieve for 15 minutes.

Combine the rice and water in a pot over low heat. Simmer for 15 to 20 minutes, stirring to prevent it from burning. When the rice is soft, stir in the black sesame paste and remove from heat.

Serve in a bowl and garnish with pine nuts. Add salt and sugar as desired. Mix everything together and enjoy.

Pot | Total time 25 min
❄ Not including marinating time

Ingredient Note

Black sesame paste
You can buy black sesame paste in Asian and Korean markets or online.

TIP

Before adding the sesame seed paste to the pot, dissolve it with some porridge

If you mix a bit of hot porridge into the sesame paste before adding it into the pot, it will mix in smoothly.

Mixed Rice with Ground Beef and Bean Sprouts

The combination of bean sprouts, sesame and ground beef is delicious, especially with the sauce. This recipe requires a rice cooker.

[Serves 4]

14 oz (400 g) bean sprouts
1½ cups (275 g) uncooked short grain rice
2 teaspoons sesame oil
7 oz (200 g) ground beef
Ⓐ 1 teaspoon minced garlic
| 2 teaspoons soy sauce
Ⓑ 4 tablespoons sake or rice wine
| ½ teaspoon salt
Scant 2 cups (450 ml) water
Super Tasty Sauce (see page 18)
Roasted sesame seeds, to garnish (see page 86)

Discard the tails and husks of the bean sprouts. Rinse and drain the rice and let it stand in a fine sieve for 15 minutes.

Heat the sesame oil in a frying pan over medium heat and add the ground beef. Fry until the meat breaks up, then stir in the ingredients in **Ⓐ**.

Put the rice and the **Ⓑ** ingredients in a rice cooker. Add the water and stir. Lay the seasoned meat and the bean sprouts on top of the rice, then turn on the rice cooker as usual. When it is done, serve the rice in bowls and top with Super Tasty Sauce and a sprinkling of roasted sesame seeds.

Pot	Total time
	15 min

※ Not including time for cooking the rice

Tip

Give it a shot! Steaming rice in a Korean stone pot is surprisingly easy

Rice is more delicious when steamed in a traditional Korean stone pot. The grains become fuller and it becomes fluffier.

Add equal quantities of rice and water by volume. Also place the other ingredients in the pot. Cover and bring to a boil over medium-high heat. Once it boils, reduce the heat to low and cook for 11 minutes, then turn the heat to high for 30 seconds. Remove from heat. Leave the lid on and allow rice to steam for 10 minutes, and then stir.

Five-grain Rice with Chestnuts

Glutinous rice gives this highly nutritious dish a delightfully springy texture, while the chestnuts and other grains like barley and millet add complex flavors.

[Serves 4]

1½ cups (275 g) uncooked short grain rice

1½ cups (275 g) uncooked glutinous rice

4 tablespoons five-grain rice mix (See Ingredient Note at right)

2½ cups (625 ml) water

1 teaspoon salt

12 shelled chestnuts

2 tablespoons goji berries (wolf-berries), optional

Wash the white rice and glutinous rice together and drain in a fine sieve. Briefly rinse the five-grain rice mix and drain.

Combine the water, rice and salt in a rice cooker and stir lightly. Place the shelled chestnuts and goji berries on top of the rice, then cook the rice using the usual setting. Gently mix all ingredients together before serving.

Ingredient Note

Five-grain rice

Five-grain rice is a mix of grains including black rice, barley, pressed barley, common millet and foxtail millet. The mixture is high in fiber as well as vitamins and minerals. You can buy five-grain rice mix in Asian and Korean markets or online.

Get a variety of nutrients with a five-grain rice blend!

You can also steam this dish in a stone pot instead of using a rice cooker. Combine the rice, glutinous rice, five-grain mix, water and salt in the pot and stir. Add the chestnuts and goji berries on top. For further steaming instructions, see the sidebar on the opposite page.

Pot

Total time
6 min

※ Not including time for cooking the rice

Pot | Total time 25 min

Chilled Buckwheat Noodles with Toppings

The superb taste of cold buckwheat noodles coated in sweet and spicy *gochujang*. Divine

[Serves 4]

½ medium daikon radish (about 14 oz/400 g), peeled

1 small carrot, peeled

A 2 tablespoons rice vinegar
1 teaspoon salt

2 hard-boiled eggs

½ apple

4 oz (125 g) store-bought *char siu* roasted pork or cooked Black Forest ham

B 8 tablespoons *gochujang* red chili bean paste
2 tablespoons rice vinegar
1 tablespoon sesame oil
1 tablespoon soy sauce
2 teaspoons sugar

12 oz (340 g) dry buckwheat noodles (*naengmyeong* or soba)

Red chili pepper threads, to garnish

Use a peeler or mandoline to shred the daikon radish and carrot. Combine in a bowl with the ingredients from **A** and let stand for 10 minutes. Drain well and squeeze to remove excess liquid.

Cut the boiled eggs in half. Thinly slice the apple and *char siu* pork or ham.

Mix the ingredients from **B** together well to make the dressing.

Bring water to a boil in a large pot. Cook the buckwheat noodles according to the directions on the noodle package. When they are cooked, plunge them in cold water and then drain well. Divide the noodles among four individual serving dishes. Arrange the vegetables, egg, apple and pork on top of each serving and drizzle the dressing on top. Garnish with red pepper threads as desired.

TIP

Mix everything together before eating

Mixing the toppings, noodles and sauce together thoroughly is the Korean way to eat a dish like this. The noodles, toppings, and seasonings mingle together and the flavors are enhanced.

Kong-guksu Chilled Soy Milk Soup with Noodles

This smooth, rich soy-milk soup with cold noodles looks as refreshing as it tastes!

[Serves 4]

Ⓐ 2 cups (500 ml) water
   1 teaspoon salt, or to taste
   4 teaspoons beef stock powder
1 Japanese cucumber or baby cucumber
3 cups (750 ml) chilled soy milk
12 oz (340 g) dry buckwheat noodles
      (*naengmyeong* or soba)
4 sweet cherries
Toasted sesame seeds, to garnish

Saucepan   Pot   Total time 25 min

Combine the ingredients from Ⓐ in a saucepan over medium heat and bring to a boil, then turn off the heat. Allow it to cool slightly, then place in the refrigerator to chill.

Cut the cucumber into matchsticks.

Stir the soy milk into the chilled beef stock broth.

Cook the buckwheat noodles according to the directions on the package. When they are cooked, plunge them into cold water, then drain well. Divide the noodles into individual serving bowls, ladle the soy milk broth over each bowl and garnish with the cucumbers and the cherries. Sprinkle some toasted sesame seeds on top and serve.

Ingredient Note

Soy milk is high in isoflavones, which provide several health benefits. Soy milk also contains ingredients like lecithin, which helps to prevent blood clots, and high-quality protein.

All you have to do is stir the soup and soy milk! This recipe is unexpectedly quick and easy

The soup for this dish is made by dissolving beef stock powder in water, cooling it, and mixing in the soy milk. It's that easy!

TIP

Udon Noodles in a Soothing Broth

If you can find them, use freshly-made wheat noodles or pasta for this dish.

[Serves 4]

1 small zucchini

4 green onions (scallions)

 5 cups (1.25 liters) Korean-style Fish Stock (see page 19), or dashi stock made from instant dashi stock powder
1 teaspoon minced garlic
1 teaspoon salt, or to taste

1¼ lbs (600 g) fresh or frozen udon noodles or 12 oz (340 g) dried udon

2 eggs, beaten

1 sheet *gim* seasoned nori, cut into thin strips

¼ teaspoon freshly ground black pepper

Slice the zucchini into thin half-moons. Thinly slice the white parts of the green onions on the diagonal.

Bring the ingredients from  to a boil in a pot. Add the noodles and boil for one minute less than the noodle package recommends. Then add the zucchini and green onion, and simmer on low heat for 1 to 2 minutes. Add in the raw egg while stirring.

Once the egg cooks, remove the pot from the heat. Serve in individual bowls. Garnish with thin strips of seaweed and sprinkle some black pepper on top.

Pot — Total time 15 min

TIP

Boiling the noodles directly in the soup thickens it

The traditional way to make this dish is to boil the noodles directly in the stock. Using handmade noodles that are dusted with flour helps thicken the soup and gives it a rich flavor—a double benefit.

Tip

Using fresh wheat noodles produces a thicker soup, which is more authentically Korean

The Korean name for this dish is Kal-guksu. *Kal* means "knife," and *guksu* means "noodles." Kal-guksu refers to handmade noodles that are cut with a knife. Try to find freshly-made wheat noodles near you!

Spicy Sausage Ramen

Using chicken hot dogs and fish cakes or tofu makes for a lighter stew than using pork or Spam, which is what Koreans normally use. This dish is popular with Korean students because it's easy to make and very filling.

[Serves 4]

4 chicken hot dogs

4 fried Japanese fish cakes or tofu cakes

6 cups (1.5 liters) water

4 packages instant ramen (soy sauce flavor)

2 tablespoons *gochujang* red chili bean paste

2 cups (200 g) roughly chopped cabbage

4 green onions (scallions), white parts only, thinly sliced on the diagonal

1½ cups (250 g) cabbage kimchi

Scant 1 cup (100 g) grated mild cheese

Cut the hot dogs diagonally into thin slices. Cut the fish cakes or tofu into slices at an angle.

Bring the water to a boil in a pot and add the hot dogs and fish cakes or tofu. Break the ramen noodles and add to the pot. Mix in the *gochujang*.

Add the cabbage and green onion and lightly simmer until done. Turn off the heat and add the instant ramen soup seasoning from just two of the packages. Stir well.

Ladle into individual bowls. Top each one with kimchi and sprinkle grated cheese over.

 You can find fried Japanese or Thai fish cakes in Asian grocery stores, either refrigerated or in the freezer section.

TIP

Break up the ramen noodles before adding them to the soup

The soup will already be full of other ingredients when you add the noodles. Break them up first to keep the pot from overflowing.

Pot

Total time
20 min

Frying Pan

Total time
15 min

Wait until the very end to add the chives so they stay deliciously crunchy!

Kimchi Fried Noodles

Kimchi works great with fried noodles. You can add any sort of meat and vegetables to this dish that you have available.

[Serves 4]

2 cups (200 g) bean sprouts
4 large cabbage leaves
Small handful of chives or 2 thin
    green onions (scallions)
1¼ cups (200 g) cabbage kimchi
2 teaspoons sesame oil
7 oz (200 g) pork loin, thinly sliced
Salt and pepper, to taste
12 oz (340 g) dry wheat noodles or
    12 oz (340 g) dry soba noodles or
    spaghetti cooked according to the
    instructions on the package
5 tablespoons water
1 teaspoon soy sauce
1 teaspoon Worcestershire sauce

Remove the tails and husks from the bean sprouts, slice the cabbage into large, square pieces and cut the chives or green onions into 1-in (2.5-cm) lengths. Cut the kimchi into small pieces.

Heat the sesame oil in the frying pan over medium heat. Fry the pork, and once it has changed color, season with the salt and pepper.

Lightly stir-fry the bean sprouts, cabbage and kimchi. Separate the noodles while adding them to the pan. Fry everything together for 2 minutes, then add 5 tablespoons of water, cover, and allow the ingredients to steam and fry.

Add the soy sauce and Worcestershire sauce and stir to evenly coat the ingredients.

This dish's flavor has a sweetness and depth to it that's not present in the usual tomato sauce pasta. Adjust the *gochujang*-to-ketchup ratio according to your preference.

Pot

Frying Pan

Total time
20 min

Korean-style Spicy Ketchup Spaghetti

You'll be hooked by the combination of *gochujang* and tomato ketchup in this grown-up sweet-and-spicy spaghetti napolitan.

[Serves 4]

14 oz (400 g) dry spaghetti

2 tablespoons vegetable oil, divided

1 white onion, peeled

½ red bell pepper, deseeded

4 hot dogs

⅔ cup (100 g) whole kernel corn

1⅓ cups (100 g) canned mushroom slices

4 tablespoons *gochujang* red chili bean paste

4 tablespoons tomato ketchup

Cook the spaghetti according to the directions on the package. Reserve 5 tablespoons of the spaghetti cooking water and drain the rest. Drizzle 1 tablespoon of the oil over the drained spaghetti and toss them to coat the noodles.

Thinly slice the onion and bell pepper into thin strips. Cut each hot dog diagonally into 10 or 12 pieces.

Heat the remaining 1 tablespoon of oil in a frying pan over medium heat. Add the onion and hot dogs and fry for 1 to 2 minutes.

Add the bell pepper and cook for another minute, then add the noodles and reserved water. Once the spaghetti separates, add the corn and mushrooms. Finally, add the *gochujang* and ketchup and cook for another minute or two, mixing the ingredients together.

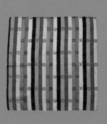

Korean-style desserts and sweets are fun! And they bring happiness!

Easy recipes—no oven needed!

Classic Korean Homemade Drinks and Sweets

Now that you have enjoyed making many different kinds of Korean dishes, you can also challenge yourself to make desserts that you'll look forward to throughout the meal! Here I'll introduce recipes for Korean sweets that you can make at home, from casual street-food snacks made with red bean paste and rice cakes with a deliciously simple sweetness to traditional sweet teas made with fruits and grains.

Yuja Citrus Jam

Yuja (or *yuzu*, in Japanese, and as it's called in the US) has a zesty citrus flavor and fragrance. Available at farmer's markets in citrus-growing regions, it is also sold online and shipped to most parts of the US. You can substitute ⅛ grapefruit, ¼ lemon, ¼ lime and ½ orange portions for the *yuja* indicated below.

[Makes about 1 pint/500 ml concentrate]

4 *yuja* or *yuzu* (14 oz/400 g total)
Sugar (half the weight of extracted juice and peels)

Halve the fruits crosswise. Squeeze out the juice and reserve. Remove the pulp and seeds from the peels with a spoon. Weigh the freshly squeezed juice. Weigh out sugar to half of the weight of the juice and peels.

 This recipe uses the *yuja* peels too, so try to use organically grown fruit, if possible.

Bring water to boil in a saucepan and add the *yuja* peels. When the water returns to a boil, take out the peels and cool on a plate. Discard the water.

This boiling process removes the impurities from the fruit.

Once the *yuja* peels have cooled, leave the inner flesh of the fruit on the peel and chop into thin strips.

Combine the *yuja* juice, sugar and sliced peels in a saucepan over high heat. Bring to a boil, then reduce heat to medium, periodically stirring the mixture from the bottom of the saucepan. Let simmer for 5 minutes to thicken into a concentrate.

Tip

Make into a tea

So much variety! Let's investigate the many uses of Yuja Citrus Jam

A hot tea made with this jam keeps the body warm and helps prevent colds. Use a ratio of about 2 tablespoons of Yuja Citrus Jam to ⅔ cup (150 ml) of hot water. Stir thoroughly and enjoy.

Spread it on bread

This jam-like mixture has a wide range of uses.

Eat it with yogurt

Pot

Total time
25 min

Sujeonggwa Dried Persimmon Punch

This traditional tea combines the spiciness of cinnamon and ginger and the sweetness of dried persimmons.

[Serves 4]

1 oz (30 g) unpeeled fresh ginger
2 cinnamon sticks
5 cups (1.25 liters) water
4–5 tablespoons brown sugar
4 small dried persimmons
1 teaspoon pine nuts

Thinly slice the ginger without peeling it. Break the cinnamon sticks in half.

Combine the ginger, cinnamon and water in a large pot over medium heat. Bring to a boil, then reduce heat to low and simmer for 15 to 20 minutes.

Remove the ginger and cinnamon sticks. Add brown sugar, to taste. Stir in the dried persimmons and simmer briefly.

Turn off the heat and let it cool. Once it is cooled, chill it in the refrigerator. Serve in cups, with one dried persimmon per serving, and sprinkle in the pine nuts just before drinking.

A Variety of Korean Teas

Aside from Yuja Citrus Jam and Sujeonggwa, Korea has many other varieties of teas with fruit and ginger.

Plum Tea (Maesil-cha)

This tea is prepared by the hot water dilution of a liquid concentrate, syrup or extract. The tangy taste is quite refreshing!

The lore says plum helps with recovering from fatigue, and people drink it when they are tired or lacking appetite. This tea has a refreshing sourness that makes it easy to drink.

Chinese Quince Tea (Mogwa-cha)

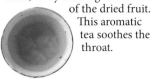

This tea is prepared by dissolving a powder or diluting a liquid concentrate or syrup in hot water, or by making an infusion of the dried fruit. This aromatic tea soothes the throat.

Chinese quince is good for the throat, especially when you have a cold. It makes a fragrant and comforting tea.

Jujube Fruit Tea (Daechu-cha)

This tea is prepared by the hot water dilution of a liquid concentrate, or by making an infusion of the dried fruit. This tea has a cozy sweetness as well as beauty benefits.

Jujube fruit tea is rich in iron and calcium. It's also supposed to reduce stress and enhance beauty. Beyond these benefits, it has a full-bodied sweetness that makes it delicious.

Magnolia Berry Tea (Omija-cha)

This tea is prepared by making a hot water infusion of the dried fruit, or by steeping the finely ground berry seeds in hot water. Enjoy the "fruit of five flavors!"

Magnolia-berry tea includes the five flavors: sweet, sour, bitter, spicy and salty. The one that is most prominent is said to depend on the drinker's physical condition. This tea is typically drunk chilled.

Sikhye

This tea is prepared by steeping cooked rice in fermented barley malt liquor and then boiling the strained liquid until it reduces to the desired sweetness. A fermented beverage with the sweetness of glutinous rice and malt.

Sikhye is said to promote digestion, so it's often drunk after a meal.

Each has its own unique taste! What a fun variety! I want to try them all!

Roasted Corn Tea (Oksusu-cha)

This tea is prepared by making a hot water infusion of corn kernels, corn silk or a combination of the two. Aromatic and sweet, and delicious cold or hot!

This tea has a distinctive, fragrant corn taste and a subtle sweetness. It is delicious warm or chilled, and is said to have diuretic effects.

Green Tea (Nok-cha)

This tea is prepared by making a hot water infusion of green tea leaves. The fragrance and taste of this green tea is well known, even outside of Korea.

This tea tastes almost the same as Japanese green tea, but is a little bit milder. It's said to soothe irritation and promote relaxation.

No cooking required

Total time
5 min

Patbingsu Sweet Shaved Ice Dessert Plate

Korean shaved ice comes with lots of toppings, including sweet red *azuki* beans, fruit and ice cream.

[Serves 4]

6 cups (840 grams) shaved ice
Any of the following, as desired:
    Canned sweet red *azuki* beans
      or bean paste
    Roasted soybean flour (*kinako*)
      or peanut powder
    Vanilla ice cream
    Cherries, kiwi, strawberries or
      other fresh or canned fruit

Put 1½ cups (210 g) shaved ice into a wide, shallow bowl and mold it into a mountain shape.

Decorate with fruit, red beans, roasted soybean flour and ice cream, and put a cherry on top.

You can buy canned sweet red *azuki* beans and roasted soybean flour in Asian and Korean markets or online.

Typically, *patbingsu* has a variety of ingredients and is mixed thoroughly before eaten. Delicious!

Stuffed Korean Hotteok Buns

These sweet Korean pancakes are a popular street food. The cinnamon and brown sugar oozes out of the center!

[Makes 4 buns]

Ⓐ ½ teaspoon dry yeast
　 1 teaspoon sugar
　 ¼ cup (65 ml) warm water
3½ oz (100 g) cake flour
Ⓑ 1 teaspoon each sesame oil and
　　　　　 roasted white sesame seeds
　 1 tablespoon sugar
2 tablespoons water
2 tablespoons brown sugar
A pinch of cinnamon
Sesame oil for shaping and frying

Frying Pan | Total time 25 min

※ Not including proofing time

Try store-bought Hotteok mix!

As with regular pancake mix, all you have to do is add water and stir—no need to let the dough rise. Some mixes also come with premade filling.

Combine the ingredients from Ⓐ in a bowl. Let stand for 15 minutes, until it bubbles.

In a separate bowl, mix the cake flour and ingredients in Ⓑ together. Add the bubbling Ⓐ ingredients and mix again. Add 2 tablespoons of water and knead until smooth. Gather it into one ball, place it in a bowl, and cover with clear plastic wrap. Allow it to proof for 30 minutes until it doubles in size.

Mix the brown sugar and cinnamon together.

Rub a few drops of sesame oil on the palm of your hand. Punch down the dough and divide into 4 pieces, then flatten one part on your palm. Place ¼ of the cinnamon sugar on the dough and wrap it up. Repeat to make four rolls.

Shape the rolls into flat circles and line them up in the pan. Heat sesame oil in a frying pan over low heat, then add the rolls and fry for 2 minutes, or until they begin to brown. Flip them over and fry for another 2 to 3 minutes. If they start puffing up, flatten them with a spatula.

TIP

Allow the dough to proof

Leave the dough to proof until it is double in size. If it doesn't rise, try setting it in a warmer place.

Oil your hands before shaping the rolls

If you put sesame oil on your palm, the dough will not stick to your hands and will be easier to handle. Place the rolls into the pan one at a time, in the same order that they were made.

Saucepan

Total time
8 min

Korean-style Sweet Red Bean Soup

The fresh sweetness of cinnamon complements candied chestnuts and candied soybeans.

[Serves 4]

12 oz (340 g) *kirimochi* (pounded rice cake)

8 candied chestnuts, walnuts or pecans

16 to 20 candied black soybeans or canned sweet red *azuki* beans

7 oz (200 g) canned *anko* sweet red bean paste

1½ cups (360 ml) water

2 tablespoons honey

Ⓐ 2 tablespoons potato starch or cornstarch

4 tablespoons water

⅛ teaspoon cinnamon

Divide the *kirimochi* into 4 portions. Cut the nuts and candied beans in half.

Place the sweet bean paste in a saucepan and little by little add the 1½ cups of water, stirring constantly. Add the honey and put the saucepan over medium heat. Thoroughly combine the Ⓐ ingredients and gradually add them to the pot, stirring constantly, to thicken.

Bring water to a boil in a separate pot and add the rice cake. Simmer for 2 to 3 minutes. Remove and place in four individual bowls.

Pour the sweet bean soup over the rice cake, add the nuts and beans, and sprinkle on some cinnamon powder.

TIP

Add the dissolved potato starch or cornstarch little by little

Heat and mix the smooth red bean paste, water and honey. Once it is warm, add in the dissolved potato starch or cornstarch Ⓐ little by little to thicken it.

You can buy *kirimochi* rice cakes, canned sweet red *azuki* beans and canned *anko* sweet red bean paste in Asian and Korean markets or online.

Makgeolli Sherbet

Turn leftover *makgeolli* rice wine (see page 17) into a tipsy dessert! Deliciously refreshing.

[Serves 4]

6 tablespoons sweetened condensed milk
½ cup (125 ml) heavy cream
1 cup (250 ml) *makgeolli* rice wine or Japanese *nigori* sake

Pour the condensed milk into a bowl. Add the heavy cream little by little, stirring constantly.

Add the *makgeolli* to the bowl and stir. Transfer the mixture to a closed container and put in the freezer. Every 1 to 2 hours, stir the mixture with a fork to prevent it from getting too hard, and return it to the freezer.

Once it is frozen to your liking, scoop it into dishes and enjoy.

No cooking required

Total time
8 min

Sweet Potato Sticks

The delightful scent and crunchy texture will keep you reaching for this simple snack!

[Serves 4]

1 Japanese sweet potato or yam
(about 7 oz/200 g total)
Cooking oil for deep-frying
2 tablespoons granulated sugar

Cut the sweet potato into thin bars. Blot with a paper towel to remove moisture.

Heat 2 in (5 cm) of oil in a deep frying pan to 340°F (170°C). Add the sweet potato and stir. Cook for 2 to 3 minutes, or until crunchy.

Take out the sweet potato sticks and set on a paper-towel-lined plate to drain. Transfer to a serving platter and sprinkle the sugar over while they are still hot.

Frying
Pan

Total time
12 min

Index

About Tuttle "Books to Span the East and West"

Our core mission at Tuttle Publishing is to create books which bring people together one page at a time. Tuttle was founded in 1832 in the small New England town of Rutland, Vermont (USA). Our fundamental values remain as strong today as they were then—to publish best-in-class books informing the English-speaking world about the countries and peoples of Asia. The world has become a smaller place today and Asia's economic, cultural and political influence has expanded, yet the need for meaningful dialogue and information about this diverse region has never been greater. Since 1948, Tuttle has been a leader in publishing books on the cultures, arts, cuisines, languages and literatures of Asia. Our authors and photographers have won numerous awards and Tuttle has published thousands of books on subjects ranging from martial arts to paper crafts. We welcome you to explore the wealth of information available on Asia at **www.tuttlepublishing.com.**

Published by Tuttle Publishing, an imprint of Periplus Editions (HK) Ltd

www.tuttlepublishing.com

ISBN 978-0-8048-5120-6

English Translation ©2019 Periplus Editions (HK) Ltd

Original Japanese title:
Ouchi de Oishii Kankoku Gohan
Copyright © 2017 Hatsue Shigenobu
English translation rights arranged with SHUFUNOTOMO Co., Ltd through Japan UNI Agency, Inc., Tokyo

[New] (page 22, 32, 38–41, 54–57, 60–61, 63, 84 and others)
Photography Tetsuro Tsuchiya (SHUFUNOTOMO Co., Ltd. Photography Department)
Styling Yukiko Ninomiya
[Reused]
Photography Yoji Yamada, Yoko Sayama (SHUFUNOTOMO Co., Ltd. Photography Department)
Styling Kayo Sakagami
Book Design Yukie Kamauchi, Kei Shimizu (GRiD)
Organization and Writing Kaori Akiyama
Illustrations Yuzuko
Co-Editor Mari Misawa
Lead Editor Yoshimi Machino (SHUFUNOTOMO Co., Ltd.)

Distributed by

North America, Latin America & Europe
Tuttle Publishing
364 Innovation Drive
North Clarendon, VT 05759-9436 U.S.A.
Tel: (802) 773-8930; Fax: (802) 773-6993
info@tuttlepublishing.com
www.tuttlepublishing.com

Asia Pacific
Berkeley Books Pte. Ltd.
3 Kallang Sector
#04-01, Singapore 349278
Tel: (65) 6741-2178; Fax: (65) 6741-2179
inquiries@periplus.com.sg
www.tuttlepublishing.com

Printed in China   1906RR

23 22 21 20 19   10 9 8 7 6 5 4 3 2 1